MOTOR CYCLES IN COLOUR

MOTOR CYCLES
IN COLOUR

by

ERIC E. THOMPSON

BLANDFORD PRESS
LONDON

First published in 1974
by Blandford Press Ltd,
167 High Holborn, London WC1V 6PH

© Blandford Press Ltd 1974
ISBN 0 7137 0711 9

Colour Plates by Colour Reproductions, Billericay
Printed and bound in Great Britain by
Tinling (1973) Ltd
Prescot and London

Contents

Acknowledgments   *page* 6

Introduction   9

The colour plates   17

The Manufacturers   97

Without the research and co-operation given to me by my son
PETER D. THOMPSON
this book would not have come to fruition.

Acknowledgments

I wish to acknowledge the generous help from so many friends who have assisted in the production of this book. My thanks to all who allowed me to photograph their magnificent machines and also to those who provided information so readily, namely: Eric Bellamy, Tommy Bullus, Jim Cairns, John Cottrell, Ivor Davies, Jack Harper, Ted Hodgdon, Eric Osborne, Harold Scott, Bob Spreadbrow, Chris Tait, Bob Thomas, and Jock West.

Thanks also to Les Shelley for his excellent line drawings and John Griffith for criticism and helpful comments. The exacting task of typing my manuscript was undertaken by Mary Day.

My grateful thanks to them all.

ERIC E. THOMPSON

Author's note

The primary purpose of this book is to convey to the reader the development of motor cycles over the years and illustrate in colour, machines that exist today, which are in most instances beautifully restored and maintained by their owners. I am deeply indebted to the owners of these machines for restoring them for others to enjoy and for making it possible for me to photograph them. Whilst every care has been taken to ensure that dates quoted are correct it must be appreciated that a date may indicate the approximate year or period of some two or three years.

It will be obvious to the reader that to attempt a complete pictorial coverage of the principal motor cycles of the world in the twentieth century in the limited space of one small volume is largely impossible. I have, therefore, attempted within the available 80 pages of colour to show a selection of the foremost models and manufacturers representative of this important industry. As I have taken all the photographs myself and have been unable to travel as widely as I would have wished, the overseas representation has, in some way, been governed by the availability of machines for photography. In some cases too an essential model within this pictorial history may have been photographed under less attractive conditions than I would wish and I must ask the forebearance of my reader if in some cases there is an unevenness of quality. My principle has been to go for the important model rather than for the glamorous photograph. Inevitably many makes that I should like to have included, have, by reason of lack of space been omitted, but the reader will, I trust appreciate that this volume purports to be an illustrated record of several decades and does not attempt to reflect the moods of a particular time.

ERIC E. THOMPSON

Introduction

The motor cycle is basically a child of the twentieth century although it was conceived in the nineteenth. Historians dispute who designed and built the first petrol-drive bicycle or tricycle. It is quite probable that Gottlieb Daimler carried out some experiments with petrol engines on a motor bicycle before he turned his attention to four wheels, but the only positive and definite claim to the honour and distinction is that of Edward Butler, an Englishman. It must be remembered that in 1884, when this machine was designed, the bicycle as it is known today had not been evolved. The standard bicycle was the 'penny-farthing' and there were a number of tricycles of various shapes and sizes.

Butler's first motor cycle, therefore, had the rather unusual appearance of single driving wheel at the rear while the driver sat between the two front wheels, which he used for steering. This machine had two horizontal cylinders which were placed on each side of the steering wheel; a curved connecting rod extended over the cylinder from the forward projecting piston-rod to the crank, which had a chain-drive connection with the back wheel. The piston-rods ran in guides to take the side thrust, while below each cylinder was a reservoir through which passed the mixture in order to heat it. Electric ignition was used, and a float feed carburettor. The valves were of the rotary type driven by chains from the driving wheel. The cylinders were water-cooled with a now most unusual sight: a water tank forming the mudguard over the rear wheel. In order to start this motor cycle, one had to raise the rear wheel by depressing a pedal on the left side which forced two small wheels down on to the ground and thereby jacked up the rear wheel. When the engine was started the rear wheel was lowered again. There were two levers on each side and slightly forward of the seat with which the driver could steer the vehicle.

The advance of the motor cycle in this country was undoubtedly greatly

9

hindered by the 'Red Flag' law, which until 1896 prohibited motor vehicles speeds in excess of four miles per hour and obliged the motorist to be preceded by a man carrying a red flag. The imagination boggles at the thought of similar restrictions enforced on the motorways today!

The turn of the century produced the first practical machines, having progressed through a period of experiments resulting in numerous attempts to provide transport. Quite naturally the pedal cycle (which had now developed into the 'safety cycle' with both wheels of similar size) was the obvious ready-made article on which to attach an engine to relieve the

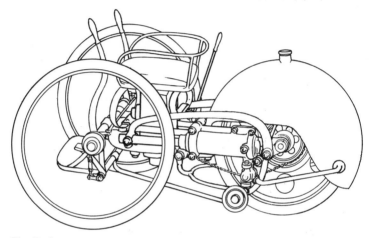

The Butler

rider of effort. It will be realised the engines had to be small and thus were considered to be of assistance rather than a completely independent form of motive power. As cycle frames and components were readily available, many enterprising firms, some quite small, purchased engines mostly from abroad, attached them to frames, adapted as they considered necessary, and offered the complete machines to a doubtful public.

Fuel and oil were vastly different from the specialised products available today. Great difficulty was experienced in starting from cold, due to oils setting in the engine necessitating frequent injections of paraffin to free the piston; poor fuel meant that vaporisation was difficult in the 'surface' type carburettors fitted at the period.

These difficulties deterred the many who looked for cheap personal transport and rather attracted young men who accepted the challenge, buying machines on which to set forth on what proved to be an adventure every time they embarked on even short journeys.

Roads at this time were rutted and abounded in sharp stones, and with horse traffic abundant, nails and flints contributed to frequent punctures in the thin cycle tyres.

The foregoing will convey to the reader that purchasers of motor cycles needed to possess a spirit of adventure as well as the price of a machine, which was about £40 to £50, a considerable sum at the beginning of this century.

Singer

With so many makers with divergent ideas, one of the basic issues was where to fix the engine. The engine inside the back wheel was successfully achieved by Perks and Birch, who took their prototype to one of the biggest cycle manufacturers of the time – Singer. Many were sold in the first few years of the century, and for those who preferred three wheels the 'Singer wheel' was fitted in the front of the tricycle. Whilst other positions were favoured by the leading makes, Werner fitted the engine over the front wheel and drove it by a twisted belt, but the obvious drawbacks were the high centre of gravity: on slippery roads, this made the machine unstable and was feared by many. Positioning the engine in the middle of the frame seems obvious today, but as pedals were considered essential for starting and assisting the engine on hills, space had to be found for both these items. Engines increased in size and performance, due in no small degree to the reliability trials organised throughout the country by the A.C.C. (Auto Cycle Club) which has subsequently to become the Auto Cycle Union.

This club later organised the acknowledged greatest road races in the world: the Tourist Trophy Races, held in the Isle of Man from 1907 to this day. As the title implies, tourism was the prime purpose promoting the event, reliability their aim and with economy very much in mind the regulations decreed that the fuel be rationed.

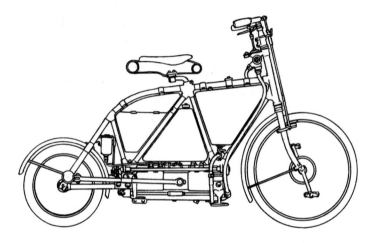

The Holden

Racing and trials have been constantly supported by manufacturers through the years, as the tests have been invaluable in advancing design, and by private competitors, who enter these events for the sheer enjoyment of riding in competitions on their chosen mounts. It is hoped to convey some idea of this development in the following pages and the story behind the production of these marvellous machines. No history of machines can be written without reference to the many men who built, rode, used or even exploited them. To deal with the last first, the name which springs to the forefront of any motor cycle enthusiast's mind is that of the larger than life character Edward Joel Pennington. There was a man who was prepared to buy and naturally sell anything, a man with the eye to the novelty both in the nature of the product involved and the method of sale. An American

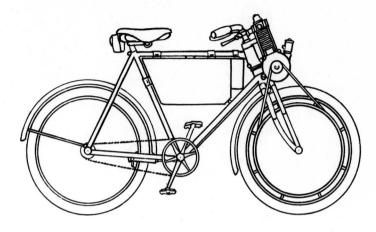

Royal Enfield

Minerva

with a certainly mixed reputation at the end of the nineteenth century, he saw the future of the salesman lay in fields mechanical. He bought and sold patents connected with motorised transport for thousands of dollars but the men he dealt with neither knew his worth nor the value of the merchandise bought. Some was mechanically sound, some worthless. The reason for his success was the selling technique of the man who might have been born in Madison Avenue. His advertising claims for motor cycles sold under his auspices included the boast that they could 'run on kerosene' and 'jump over rivers', neither of which (not surprisingly) was

Pennington

substantiated by fact. Pennington was larger than life and trod the tightrope between wealth and bankruptcy frequently but with outward calm at all times. Despite his many financial coups, he died penniless.

The men who have ridden the motor cycles may be a little less extravagant in appearance and outlook, but are perhaps more interesting to the enthusiast. Riders such as Geoff Duke, John Surtees, Mike Hailwood and Giacomo Agostini are racing men known to almost every man and boy, and not a few women. For the older reader the names of Jimmy Simpson, Alec Bennett, Charlie Collier, Stanley Woods and Graham Walker should be included where any roll of racing honour is read. Men who were riders but famous in other fields include Lawrence of Arabia (T. E. Lawrence), who had a great passion for riding his Brough Superior 'Boanerges' and describes this love for motor cycling in brilliant prose in his book *The Mint*; Sir Ralph Richardson, the great actor, and W. O. Bentley, better known for the cars he made.

There are many not so famous men whose feats of riding have endured when their names are long forgotten. Remarkable performances include the many mountain climbs made in the first few years of this century, which developed into races against the clock up Snowdon or Ben Nevis in the 1920s by men riding B.S.A. and Francis-Barnett motor cycles respectively. Extraordinary performances include the feats of the man who rode an Ariel motor cycle across the sea and another who rode a Henderson round a roller-coaster at a Californian funfair. Naturally there have been many speed and distance records achieved over the last seventy-odd years and details of these are given where appropriate throughout this book. It must be said that not all motor cycle achievements are recorded by men, and 'women's lib' would have been proud of Mrs Meeten's 1,000 miles in five days on a Francis-Barnett, Marjorie Cottle's trials exploits and Fay Taylor's impressive displays on the dirt track, all of which helped to put a 'roar' into the twenties. At about the same time two men were attracting attention in the racing circles claiming records in the Isle of Man T.T. races unlikely to ever be surpassed. The names Cowley and Applebee may not be familiar to the present-day reader, but he need not be ashamed for they were not that familiar to the motor cyclists of the time either. These two men raced fairly successfully in the T.T. races when at the age of most men's retirement from normal work. Cowley was sixty-one when he last competed and Applebee fifty-nine.

In Germany it must have been a splendid sight to witness Ernst Henne 'averaging a ton' in 1929 down a Munich autobahn on his B.M.W. For endurance records it would be hard to better the performances of Cannon-ball Baker on his Indian, crossing the USA west to east, north to south. These and many other achievements, the men who accomplished them and most importantly of all, the machines that did the work and the men who built them are dealt with in this book. It cannot be complete, but it attempts to show how some of the famous and also some of the lesser-known marques grew up in the twentieth century.

THE BAT MOTOR MANUFACTURING COMPANY LTD
BAT
PENGE LONDON

THE RALEIGH
NOTTINGHAM
ENGLAND

LEVIS
LEVIS ET CELER

TRIUMPH
TRIUMPH
CYCLE C° L™
COVENTRY

ROYAL ENFIELD
MADE LIKE A GUN
TRADE MARK
THE ENFIELD CYCLE C° L™
REDDITCH.

DUNELT
SHEFFIELD

EXCELSIOR
TRADE MARK
EXCELSIOR MOTOR C° L™
BIRMINGHAM
FOUNDED IN COVENTRY 1874
MADE IN ENGLAND

GLORIA
TRIUMPH CYCLE C° L™
COVENTRY

New Imperial
MOTORS L™
BIRMINGHAM ENG.

"Indian" Motocycle
THE Hendee Manufacturing C°

ABC
Sopwith
AVIATION & ENGINEERING
Co. L™.

1A   ABC. This rare 1913 model 500cc horizontally opposed twin with hub type gear fitted in the frame.

1B   ABC. A Sopwith-made 398cc HO twin-engine gearbox unit in a spring frame.

1C ABC. 'Skootamota' designed by Granville Bradshaw, powered by single-cylinder engine with direct chain drive.

1D ABC. This racing version has a shorter frame than 1 B, but engine unit is similar.

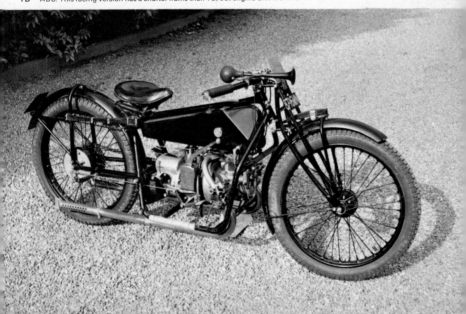

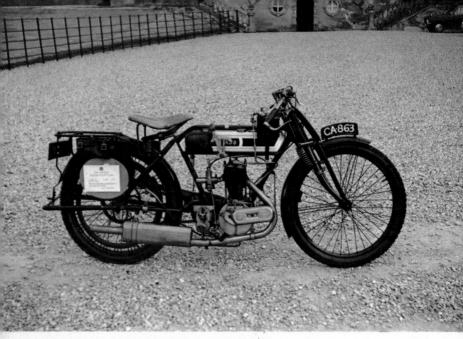

2A   A.J.S. This racing machine finished 4th in the Junior T.T. of 1914.

2B   A.J.S. Model K7, a production racing machine, with chain-driven overhead camshaft engine of 350cc capacity.

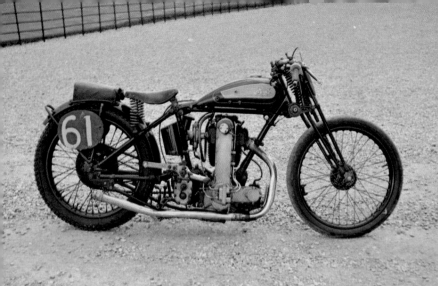

2C A.J.S. This model M10 is a Brooklands Special with overhead camshaft engine.

2D A.J.S. A 1950 edition of the 'Boy Racer' 7R. The overhead camshaft engine is of 350cc. Produced from 1948 to 1962.

3A ARIEL. A 1914 racing model. The engine is a side valve White and Poppe, and direct belt is employed.

3B ARIEL. A 1925 500cc side-valve machine with all chain drive. The lighting is acetylene.

3C ARIEL. An example of the famous 'Square four' of 1000cc. Some early models were of 600cc.

4A ASCOT PULLIN. A luxury mount bristling with innovations, made in 1928. The pressed steel frame carries a 500cc OHV engine.

5A BAT This 1910 model is fitted with 770cc J.A.P. engine. A touring sidecar is fitted.

5B BAT A 1913 machine with Armstrong hub gear in rear wheel, driven by belt.

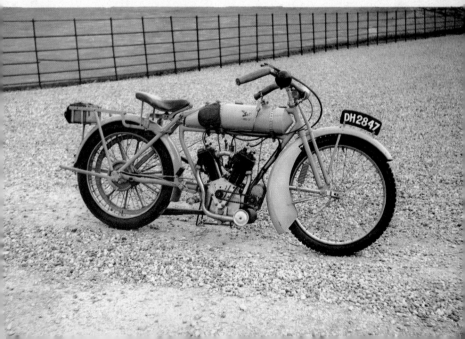

6A B.M.W. This factory has made H.O. twins from the 1920s until today. 500cc to 900cc engines are used.

7A BROUGH SUPERIOR. George Brough's famous racing machine 'Old Bill'. With this 1000cc engine he achieved many wins in hill climbs and sprints.

7B BROUGH SUPERIOR. The Alpine Grand Sports of 1925 with the 984cc OHV J.A.P. engine.

7C BROUGH SUPERIOR. A Sprint special built in 1927 with the 8-55 J.A.P. engine. This machine exceeded 122 m.p.h. on sand.

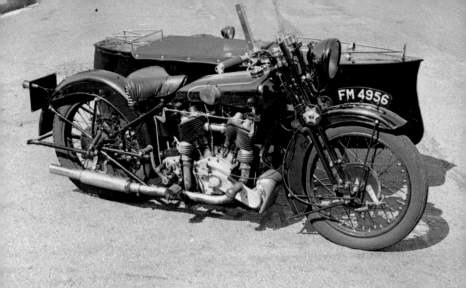

7D   BROUGH SUPERIOR. A 1928 model SS80 de Luxe with Watsonian launch sidecar. The engine is a 980cc J.A.P.

7E   BROUGH SUPERIOR. The 1932 four cylinder fitted with 'Austin 7' engine and gearbox, with reverse gear! Twin rear wheels are fitted.

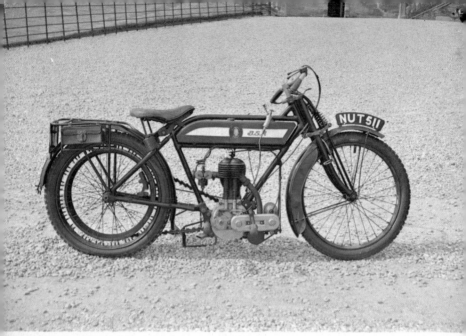

8A   B.S.A. A 1913 'TT' model devoid of pedals which featured on standard models. Direct belt drive is employed.

8B   B.S.A. The 'Big Twin' sidecar outfit, a popular choice of the family man in 1921.

8C   B.S.A. A 250cc 'Round Tank' 1926 version. Adopted by the G.P.O. for telegram delivery.

8D   B.S.A. A touring 350cc side-valve model of 1924. A 3-speed gearbox is fitted.

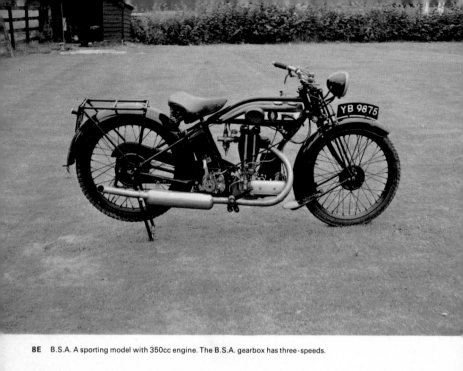

8E   B.S.A. A sporting model with 350cc engine. The B.S.A. gearbox has three-speeds.

8F   B.S.A. An example of the 'Star' range. A 1936 edition with a good performance.

9A CALTHORPE. The 'Ivory Calthorpe' of 1930 was a striking machine – fitted with 500cc o.h.v. engine of their own manufacture.

10A CHATER LEA. The 350cc o.h.v. Blackburne engine was fitted in 1923. A lively sporting mount.

11A   COTTON. This Sprint special, built in 1930, is fitted with a 500cc o.h.v. Blackburne engine.

12A   D.K.W. This unusual 1938 racing model has a 350cc supercharged engine with 5 pistons.

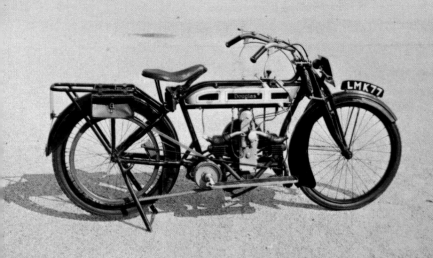

13A DOUGLAS. A 1913—2¾h.p. model horizontally-opposed twin 'two speeder' as used by D.R.s in the First World War.

13B DOUGLAS. A 1914 racing version 2¾h.p. model with two-speed gears and belt final drive.

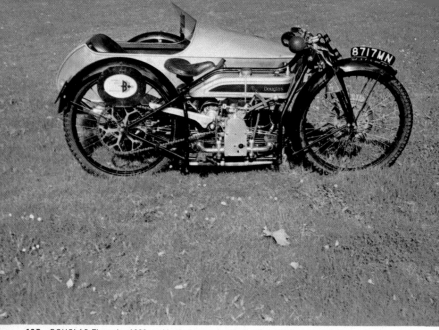

13C DOUGLAS. The racing 1923 machine had an overhead valve 'flat twin' engine of 500cc. Note 'research' brakes (see no. 56).

13D DOUGLAS. A 1928, 500cc o.h.v. horizontally opposed twin racing model. A modified version was successfully used on the cinder tracks.

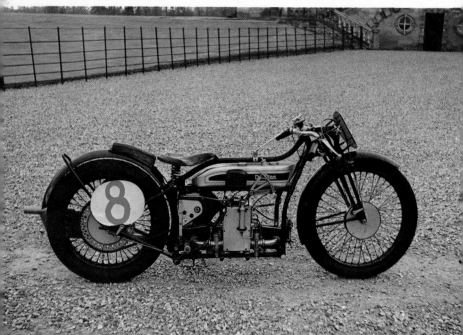

13E DOUGLAS. The 'Endeavour' of 1934 had a 494cc s.v. engine and its many unusual features included shaft drive.

13F DOUGLAS. The Mark III de Luxe, a 348cc – 180° twin with a claimed speed of over 80 m.p.h.

14A DREADNOUGHT. Built in 1902/3 with a 3½ h.p. M.M.C. engine and direct belt drive. One of the earliest examples of a 'special'

15A EXCELSIOR. This is a fine example of the 'Manxman' with the 350 overhead camshaft engine of their own manufacture.

16A FRANCIS BARNETT. The 1928 'straight tube' frame model has a Villiers 147cc and two-speed Albion gearbox.

17A GILERA. The Saturno model of 1951 was a racing special with single cylinder o.h.v. engine.

18A   HARLEY DAVIDSON. The 1919 example has overhead inlet valves and side exhaust. The clutch interlocks with the gearbox.

18B   HARLEY DAVIDSON. No front brake was fitted until the twenties.

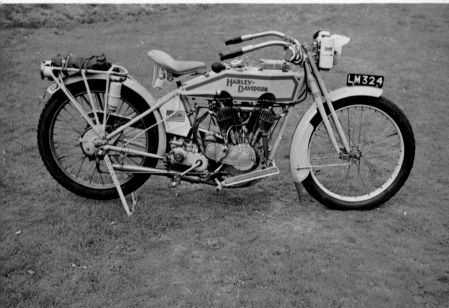

18C   HARLEY DAVIDSON. Overhead inlet valves needed tank cutaways.

18D   HARLEY DAVIDSON. A 1929 model 'J' with 998cc Vee-twin engine, the last year the inlet over exhaust system was used. Used by many police forces in USA.

19A HENDERSON A powerful machine with four cylinder engine of 1200cc which tended to dwarf most machines of the vintage period.

20A   HONDA. A racing 125cc model CR93 using an eight-valve twin-cylinder engine with double overhead camshafts.

20B   HONDA. Another specialist machine — this one for trail riders.

20C HONDA. Similar power unit to the trail — this is in 'everyday' guise.

20D HONDA. A sports roadster with twin-cylinder engine.

20E HONDA. The 750 'four' with modified forks for sidecar use.

21A H.R.D. A 1927 model with o.h.v. J.A.P. engine similar to the machine used by F. W. Dixon to win the Junior T.T. of that year.

21B VINCENT H.R.D. The 1000cc British o.h.v. Vee-twin with unorthodox spring frame.

22A HUMBER. The 'Beeston' was a popular machine in 1902 fitted with a 372cc engine.

22B HUMBER. A lightweight machine made in 1911 with a 192cc engine.

22C HUMBER. In 1928 this 350cc overhead camshaft engine was of their own manufacture.

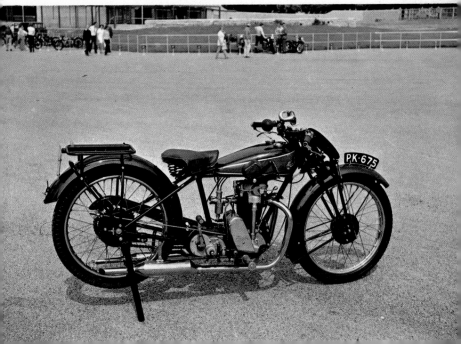

23A HUSQVARNA A 1933 popular Swedish single cylinder model with 3-speed gearbox.

24A   INDIAN. This 4-cylinder 'in line' was a development from the acquired Henderson concern.

24B   INDIAN. This example of the Four has a 1265cc engine produced in 1934.

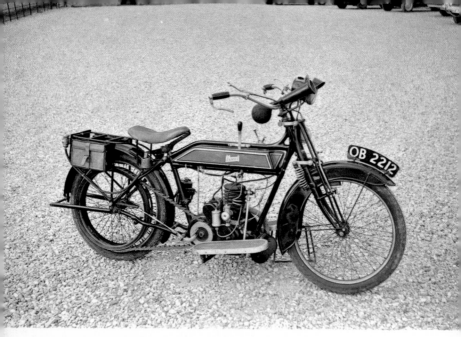

25A   JAMES. A popular lightweight in 1914 with 2-speed gear and engine of 225cc.

25B   JAMES. A 1913 touring mount with 500cc side valve engine. Note complete enclosure of chains.

25C JAMES. A 1925 Vee-twin side valve engine, 3-speed gearbox and all-chain drive. An overhead valve edition was also marketed.

26A KAWASAKI. A 500cc three cylinder two-stroke—fast and thirsty.

27A   LEA FRANCIS. A 430cc J.A.P. engine is fitted to this 1914 model. The chains are completely enclosed.

27B   LEA FRANCIS. This 1921 model is fitted with the Swiss M.A.G. engine.

28A LEVIS. One of the most popular lightweights. A 1926 model with 247cc two-stroke engine.

29A MARTINSYDE. Only a small quantity of these machines were made by the Martinsyde Aircraft Co. in 1922.

30A MATCHLESS. The model 8B of 1914 was a luxury touring outfit. A large M.A.G. engine is used.

30B MATCHLESS. The G3C was a popular 'Trials' machine. A 350cc engine is used in a spring frame.

31A MORGAN. An early example of the most successful three wheeler. This one, made in 1913, has an air-cooled J A P engine.

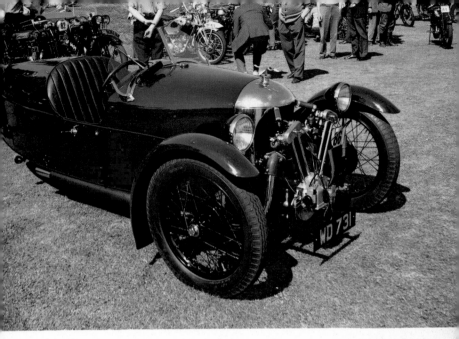

31B MORGAN. This 'Aero' is fitted with an o.h.v. J.A.P. engine.

31C MORGAN. A 1933 'Aero' model, fitted with a 'Matchless' engine.

32A   MOTO GUZZI. A racing 'four valve' single with o.h.c. engine. Only a few of these were made in 1929.

32B   MOTO GUZZI. This machine was successfully raced by Maurice Cann. It is a 250cc o.h.c. single.

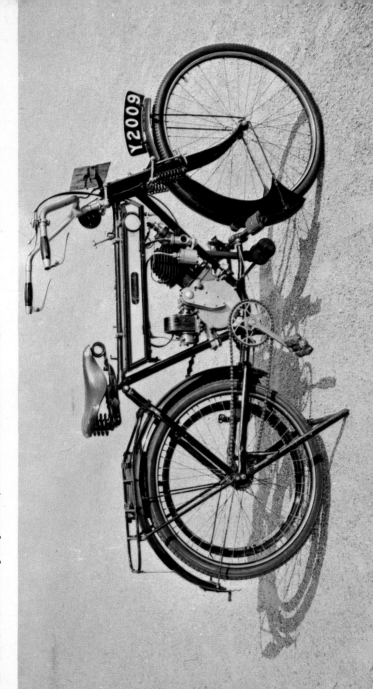

33A MOTOSACOCHE. A true lightweight of the day. This 1913 model had a 290cc side valve engine.

34A NORTON. A Peugeot 5 h.p. engine is fitted to this machine which is reputed to have won the twin

34B NORTON. These sporting 490cc side valve models were capable of 80 m.p.h. Direct belt drive is used.

34C   NORTON. The 16H model was listed for over forty years, this being a 1925 edition.

34D   NORTON. The 'International' had a 490cc o.h.c. engine. This is a 1932 machine.

34E NORTON. The ES2 had an o.h.v. 490cc engine. This one is fitted with an 'International' tank, an optional extra.

34F NORTON. The 'Featherbed', so named for its road holding which was a marked improvement on the 'Garden Gate' frame. An outside flywheel was only used on experimental factory models.

35A N.S.U. A 250cc racer from this famous German factory. This model is a 1957 example with double o.h.c.

36A and 36B   N.U.T. Two fine examples of these Vee-twins, made in 1925.

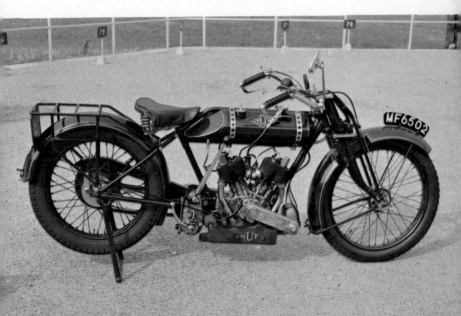

37A P. & M. This 1909 model has 469cc engine with automatic inlet valve, two speed gears with expanding clutches. All chain drive is used.

37B P. & M. A 'Panther' model of 1927 with the overhead valve engine of 499cc. A 4-speed gearbox was employed.

was very advanced in 1914.

39A RUDGE 'MULTI'. 1912 the first year this model was introduced, continuing until 1923. The multi-gear

39B   RUDGE 'MULTI'. 1915 edition the 499cc engine being similar to the earlier model, but modified frame gave lower riding position—a direct result of a 1914 T.T. victory.

39C   RUDGE WHITWORTH. These 'Dirt Track' models enjoyed considerable success on the speedway 1928-1930. The o.h.v. engine had a four-valve head.

39D RUDGE WHITWORTH. This 250cc example was similar to the machine with which Graham Walker won the Lightweight T.T. in 1931.

39E RUDGE WHITWORTH. A 350cc four-valve four-speed racing machine of 1930.

39F RUDGE WHITWORTH. The 'Ulster' model, so named after the success in the 1928 Ulster Grand Prix.

40A   SCOTT. This 1929 Flying Squirrel carried its owner 200,000 miles, many on the Continent of Europe.

40B   SCOTT. A 'Sprint Special' 596cc twin-cylinder water-cooled two-stroke.

41A SINGER. A touring machine with 3½ h.p. side-valve engine, made in 1915, although of a rather earlier period, typical of the period.

42A SUNBEAM This 1914 model has a J.A.P. 770cc engine. A luxury passenger outfit of its day.

42B SUNBEAM. A T.T. replica of 3½ h.p. similar to the machine which won the Senior T.T. at over 50 m.p.h. in 1922.

42C SUNBEAM. The 'Light Tourist' model has a 499cc side-valve engine, both chains run in oil baths.

42D　SUNBEAM. The model '90' has a 500cc o.h.v. engine with twin port head. A super sports model.

42E　SUNBEAM. This 1928 'model 8' represents the last year of the 'flat' tank models. This 350 has a single port head.

42F SUNBEAM. The S7, produced as a luxury mount from 1946 to 1954. A vertical twin engine, shaft drive and balloon tyres.

43A SUZUKI. Model TS100 a single-cylinder two-stroke engine with rotary disc valve. A 5-speed gearbox

SUZUKI. The large three-cylinder water-cooled two-stroke machine. A super bike.

44A   TRIUMPH. This is the oldest known model of this marque, made in 1903. A J.A.P. engine is used.

44B   TRIUMPH. This Roadster of 1910 has the $3\frac{1}{2}$ h.p. side-valve engine, single-speed with hub clutch.

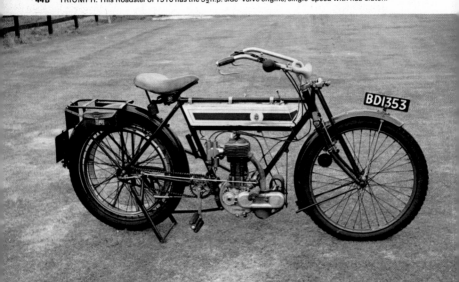

44C TRIUMPH. The 1914 T.T. model with 3½h.p. engine and direct belt drive.

44D TRIUMPH. The model 'H' as used by despatch riders during the First World War.

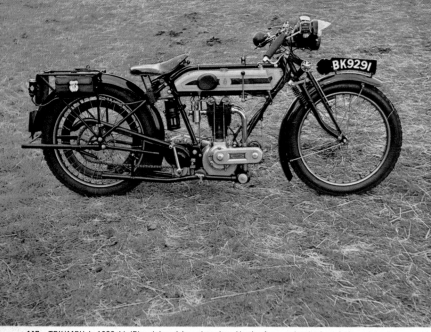

44E TRIUMPH. In 1922 this 'Ricardo' model was introduced having four overhead valves. A pleasant touring machine.

44F TRIUMPH. The 'Speed Twin' with the parallel vertical twin o.h.v. engine. As used extensively by police forces throughout the world.

44G   TRIUMPH. A 'Grand Prix' racing machine 500cc prepared for the Manx Grand Prix in 1948, and being rebuilt as we go to press.

44H   TRIUMPH. The 'Trident' a 750cc engine with three parallel cylinders, five-speed gearbox and disc brake on front wheel. Capable of over 110 m.p.h.

45A TRUMP. This racing monster, with 1000cc 90 bore J.A.P. engine, was built by F. A. McNab in 1910, to

46A VAUXHALL. This outstanding machine built by the car firm in 1922 has a four-cylinder engine and shaft drive.

47A   VELOCETTE. A 1919 211cc two-stroke engined machine, it has a 2-speed gearbox.

47B   VELOCETTE. A 1922 Racing model two-stroke as raced in the T.T. Races of 1921 and 1922, gaining 3rd place in each.

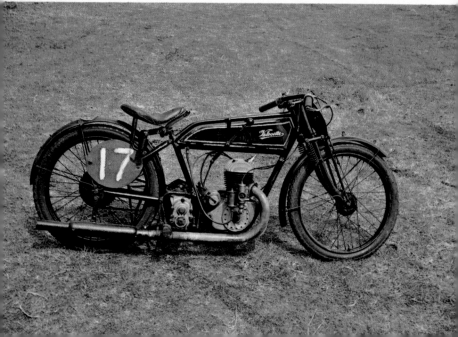

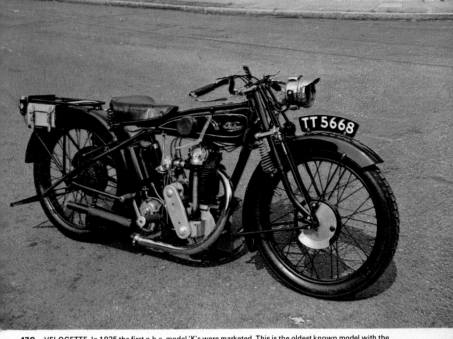

47C VELOCETTE. In 1925 the first o.h.c. model 'K's were marketed. This is the oldest known model with the o.h.c. – 350cc engine.

47D VELOCETTE. A 1931 KTT model, the production o.h.c. racing machine, with 3-speed gearbox.

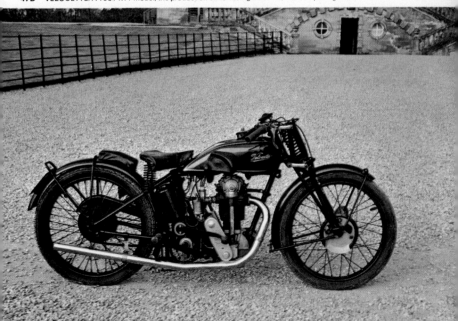

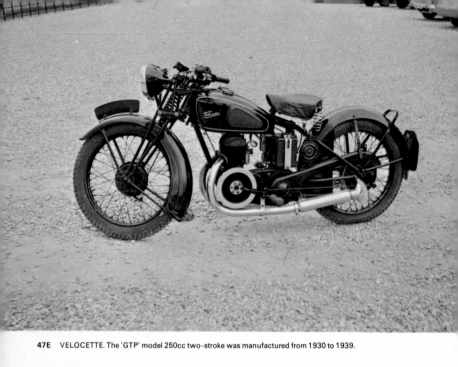

47E   VELOCETTE. The 'GTP' model 250cc two-stroke was manufactured from 1930 to 1939.

47F   VELOCETTE. 1947 MSS, a 500cc push-rod o.h.v. engine, with 'prewar' specification.

47G VELOCETTE. 200cc Vogue with water-cooled flat twin engine and shaft drive. The bodywork is fibre glass.

47H VELOCETTE. This Thruxton model was ridden to victory in the 1967 Production T.T.

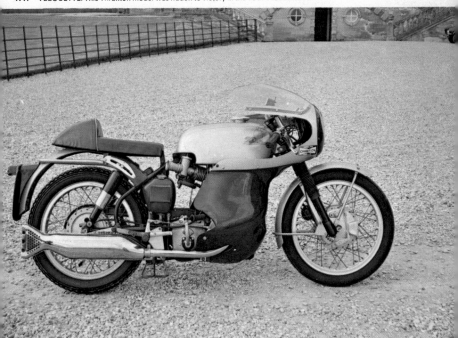

48A   WOOLER   This is the earliest example of this make, a 344cc two-stroke made in 1911.

49A   YAMAHA. One of the many models offered by this Japanese factory.

50A ZENITH. The famous 'Gradua', this 1914 model has 6 h.p. J.A.P. engine.

50B ZENITH. A 1926 combination with 680cc Vee-twin J.A.P. engine and Sturmey-Archer gearbox.

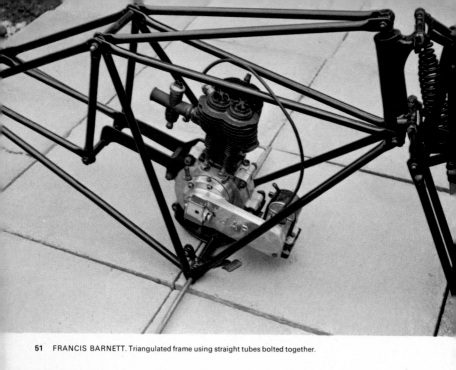

51 FRANCIS BARNETT. Triangulated frame using straight tubes bolted together.

52 P &M. Method of engine replacing front down tube. Used from 1900 to 1966.

53 VELOCETTE. Overhead camshaft engine produced from 1925 to 1948 with modification.

54 J.A.P. 'Four cam' side-valve 85·5 × 85 mm engine as fitted to many makes of machines including three and four wheelers.

55 SIDECAR. This wicker body was light and strong; very popular before the First World War.

56 SIDECAR. The banking sidecar was designed by F. W. Dixon for the first sidecar T.T. race in 1923, which he won.

1 A.B.C.

Granville Bradshaw first designed and completed the construction of motor cycles for the 'All British (Engine) Company' in 1913.

The frame consisted of brazed tubes and flat steel strip with leaf spring rear suspension. The engine was a horizontally-opposed twin-cylinder placed fore and aft in the frame with side inlet and overhead exhaust valves and a total capacity of 500cc. The gear 'box' was in fact a hub gear by Armstrong with three speeds mounted behind the engine as in later conventional countershaft boxes with all chain-drive. Front brakes were of the stirrup type on the Druid forks but an external contracting band brake was used on the rear wheel. Similar machines were made in 1914, and at the outbreak of war production of motor cycles ceased but the engines were used for a variety of purposes, one being to pump water out of the trenches in France.

It was not until after the First World War that Bradshaw revolutionised the motor cycle industry with the 398cc machine with its over-square flat twin engine in unit with a four-speed gearbox, mounted transversely in a wide cradle frame with leaf springing front and rear. In 1918 T. O. M. Sopwith, with 3,500 employees to occupy (and the large demand for aeroplanes at an end with the conclusion of the war), turned his attention to motor cycle manufacture and Granville Bradshaw. The latter promised a prototype within three weeks to the disbelief of Sopwith, who agreed to manufacture the same when ready, but to back up this disbelief he made a wager that for each day earlier than three weeks he would give Granville Bradshaw £100 and conversely for each day after three weeks Granville Bradshaw would give him £100. Granville Bradshaw came out with £1,000 from that little matter!

The motor cycle was designed with the accent on comfort and convenience, with legshields and under-tray to allow the city man to ride without a change of clothing. It was compact and relatively light in weight. Rear springing was an innovation and a unique design of a full loop frame having a horizontally-opposed twin engine with turned steel cylinders (as in aircraft practice) was mounted across the frame with overhead valves and this made the machine a highly desirable vehicle, which could be ordered finished in grey or black paint.

Unfortunately the motor cycle, which attracted all the attention in its field for its approach to design, struck financial hazards which it found impossible to overcome. Originally intended for sale at a price of £70 in 1919, it soon became apparent that a retail price of £160 was more realistic and from the manufacturers' viewpoint a price under £300 was not going to bring them any profit. The large waiting list was never satisfied, so the enthusiasts not unnaturally turned their attention to less expensive machines and in 1921 the Sopwith factory closed down, after having made about 3,300 machines.

This machine could have been the most famous motor cycle of all time had its various faults been cured, but unhappily this was not to be. The valve gear, a weak feature of design, was rectified by firms offering alternative components, yet for A.B.C. the end came in 1923.

The French firm of Gnome Rhone manufactured a modified version of the machine under licence up to 1925 and a few of these are still running in various parts of the world. Fortunately a number of Sopwith machines are also still running and give great pleasure to their enthusiastic owners.

2 A.J.S.

This is another British manufacturer with a history of achievement over seventy years but unlike many of its former contemporaries it has adapted to the present day needs. Not, it should be added without amalgamation with another well-known make, but the name still lingers on and the influence remains behind the name.

The brothers Stevens – Harry, George, Jack and Joe were so to speak in motor cycle manufacturing from the beginning. As early as 1897 all four had combined to make a motorbicycle from a bicycle frame to which they attached a petrol tank and Mitchell engine and of course a belt-drive for the rear wheel. It was perhaps not unnatural that there should be a high percentage of the family interested in engineering matters as their father was a precision engineer. Perhaps with his encouragement and more than probably with his inherited ability and aptitude the birth of one of Britain's great motor cycle names took place in Wednesfield near Wolverhampton in the midlands of England. They continued to make motor cycles and supply various other manufacturers with their products thereafter, but it was not until 1909–1910 that a completely original A.J.S. was constructed and put on the market.

It was about this time that the T.T. race in the Isle of Man was split into two categories: 500cc Senior and 350cc Junior events. The original A.J.S. was a 298cc two-speed belt-driven motor cycle and entered in the Junior event of 1911. The name A.J.S. was taken from the initials of the eldest brother Albert John (Jack) Stevens, probably because he was the senior partner – in age! By 1912 chain-drive had been introduced to A.J.S. machines and it was not long after that the brothers had their first success in the T.T. – and therefore felt they had made their mark in the motor cycle world – with a wonderful first and second place in the Junior race of 1914. That same year the brothers moved their premises to Graiseley House, Wolverhampton. During the war the factory turned out munitions, but with the ceasefire, returned with a vengeance to the manufacture of success- ful motor cycles. 1920 saw the introduction of overhead valves which proved a great success on lightweight bikes. A 350cc A.J.S. won the 1920 Junior and the following year went one better by taking both Junior and Senior T.T.s. Howard Davies, who later went into business with his own H.R.D., was the rider in the latter event, having taken second place in the Junior. This achievement can never be repeated as the Senior is now prohibited to motor cycles under 350cc.

The progress of A.J.S. has been interjected with four outstanding models. The first of these was the 'Big Port' introduced in the early 1920s which was modified over the next decade in many ways. Initially a development of the successful Junior T.T. winner of 1920, it was later developed as a 500cc when it became the first machine to lap the T.T. course at 70 m.p.h., with Jimmy Simpson in the saddle. A few years earlier the same rider had been the first to lap in the Junior at 60 m.p.h., again on an A.J.S. By 1929 the A.J.S. held over a hundred world records which itself must be a record! The Stevens brothers aimed at yet another – the world land speed record – and with infinite care prepared a 1000cc V-twin designed by Ike Hatch. Unhappily it returned a disappointing 121 m.p.h. and was abandoned for the next few years until new found enthusiasm caused it to be taken out again and metaphorically dusted down before returning, after the fitting of a supercharger, yet another 'failure' at 132 m.p.h. average when the record stood at just over 150 m.p.h.

But things had changed in that intervening period for A.J.S., namely a small matter of temporary liquidation before being taken over by the makers of Matchless, H. Collier and Sons. With the take-over came a move to London into the Plumstead area. But motor cycles of truly A.J.S. design and manufacture continued to be produced. The trading title was changed in 1938 to Associated Motorcycles Ltd, and in the fifties they absorbed three other famous makes: Norton, James and Francis-Barnett. Before the Second World War such eminent riders as Eric Williams, Jimmy Simpson and Jimmy Guthrie had achieved success on Ajays in major racing events. After the war other notable racers who chose them were Les Graham, Bob Foster, Bill Doran, Rod Coleman, Fergus Anderson, Bob McIntyre and Reg Armstrong. But it was not in the racing circle that A.J.S. really hit the jackpot; their forte was more in the world of reliability trials demonstrated by expert riders like Hugh Viney and Gordon Jackson. Between 1947 and 1961 these two riders each won the Scottish Six Days' Trial four times with several 'placings' on other occasions and in that period on two occasions the manufacturers award was won by A.J.S. It may well have been this background of success that led eventually to the Y4 250cc moto-cross successes. For it is in that quarter that A.J.S. next found reward and over the latter part of the 1960s in hands of the likes of Malcolm Davis the little Ajay has won new fame which resulted in a factory opening in the United States of America to manufacture this popular product.

Between times, so to speak, the other two outstanding models have been the 'Porcupine' and '7R' otherwise known as the 'Boy Racer' introduced soon after the Second World War. The 499cc Porcupine was so called because its cylinder head finning was of a spikey appearance. The engine lay almost horizontally in the duplex frame with twin overhead camshafts and a feature of this model was that the engine ran 'backwards'! The 'Porcs' had a somewhat chequered career in racing even if not always the first to receive the chequered flag! On one famous occasion, temperamental as ever, two racing machines were in pieces as the third was taken for scrutineering. The time had almost expired for this essential preliminary to taking part in the Ulster Grand Prix. With great presence of mind one machine was presented to the Scrutineers three times with the different numbers of the team stuck on front and side and thereby enabled all to compete! In the 1949 Senior T.T. victory seemed assured for Les Graham, with a good lead over his rivals and only a couple of miles to ride, when the magneto armature sheared, the engine consequently gave up the struggle and the unfortunate Graham had to push the bike in to tenth place. However not all was disappointment for the Porcupine since it gave Les Graham a win in the Swiss G.P. and the European 500cc championship in 1949, the latter being the forerunner to the World Championship.

More successful than the Porcupine was the 7R which was made during the late 1940s through the 1950s and into the 1960s. This 350cc overhead camshaft machine met with early success and was popular with amateur as well as professional racing enthusiasts, on the continent of Europe as well as in Great Britain. Notable amongst the trophies won by the '7R' were several Manx Grands Prix victories, these races being open to amateur or private sponsored riders. The motor cycles are not factory specials and are perhaps therefore better examples of the factories' products since a cynic can argue that the wealth and time devoted to one machine in a particular race may not fairly reflect the time, money and thought contributed to the machines that the factory sell to the public.

Now A.J.S. has been swallowed with Associated Motorcycles Ltd into Norton Villiers Limited. Within this confinement they continue to make a name for themselves in the moto-cross field with the Y4 two-stroke model.

3 ARIEL

Ariel, symbolised by the flying horse, started its life quietly enough as a motor tricycle in 1898 and subsequently leaped into the public eye over the next fifty years until, as with so many other companies, financial needs drove it into amalgamation with other motor cycle manufacturers. The public attention was grabbed by the publicity-conscious men of Ariel with the specific aim of selling their product in a world which had become saturated with too many choices for the potential buyers.

The first Ariel tricycle was powered by a de Dion Bouton single-cylinder engine and the first Ariel motor cycle did not make its public appearance before 1902. The man metaphorically at the helm at this period of time was Charles Sangster, a man with vision and drive. Components Ltd, as it was then called, produced the Ariel motor cycle with a Kerry engine, and Sangster had them on endurance runs such as John O'Groats to Lands End (the north tip of Scotland to the south-west tip of England) with a view to proving their reliability and stamina and achieving his main purpose of attracting public attention.

One of the earliest Ariel motor cars was the first motor vehicle to ascend Mount Snowdon (1904) and gained the organisation further public acclaim. The earliest Ariel motor cycles were between 2 and $3\frac{1}{2}$ horsepower machines ranging in cost between about £35 and £50. This sum of money being the best part of the average man's income for a year meant that sales talk had to be really attractive to encourage purchasers. One such promotion in 1905 was the offer of £25 on 'any last year's models' in a part exchange deal for a new Ariel – indeed a very generous offer. Despite this magnanimous gesture Ariel sales were not greatly improved and the number of models available for purchase decreased during the next few years. By the time of the First World War the range had been made up to include a 500cc side valve single-cylinder engine model and a 6 horsepower (about 670cc) side valve V-twin, the engines being provided by courtesy of White and Poppe. A prototype 350cc two-stroke was announced but never built. After the war, efforts were concentrated on turning out the 6 and 8 horsepower twin-cylinder machines. The post-war period also saw production of a light motor car, the pride and joy of Jack Sangster, son of Charles. But the Ariel motor cycle aspect of the business was not to get its much-needed shot in the arm until 1925 when Victor Moles arrived as sales manager and decided that a complete shake up of policy and action was necessary. He and the newly installed Valentine Page, a former J.A.P. technician, pushed to one side all the models and ideas that were then in production or on the drawing board and brought out their own entirely new 550cc side valve and 500cc overhead valve models under the slogan 'Ariel – the Modern Motor Cycle'. With a guaranteed speed of about 80 m.p.h. on the sports model, the new broom swept the board clean. It is interesting to note that, despite the usual increase in the cost of living, the purchase price of the 1925 Ariel was £55, only two or three pounds more than their 1904 models. The introduction of saddle tanks and cradle frames in 1927 and semi-enclosure of overhead valves and two port engines and the triangulated side-car chassis in 1928 kept Ariel motor cycles to the forefront of British motor cycle popularity, and by 1929 they were making over a thousand motor cycles each week.

Ever keeping an eye out for publicity, Ariel became the first motor cycle to cross the English Channel – entirely under its own power. In August 1929 Harry Perrey mounted his Ariel on floats and with the back wheel driving a paddle rode across the sea to arrive in Calais 3 hours 50 minutes after he had left the English shore line. He naturally had a crew, F. Thacker, who rode on the pillion seat. Not satisfied with this Perrey improved his time on the return journey taking something like three hours, the reason for this probably being that he recognised the route on the way back! This was not the only publicity stunt pulled by the manufacturers and the newspapers were full of pictures of Ariel motor cycles being used by well-known political or threatrical personalities and it is therefore not surprising that the motor cycles used a few years later by George Formby in the famous motor cycling film *No Limit* included a not-heavily disguised Ariel.

The 1930s saw production of the Ariel models with sloping engines and the introduction of the still famous Ariel Square Four, then an overhead camshaft 500cc model. The Square Four with four-cylinder engines of 500, 600 and 1000cc were in production until 1958. The thirties were however an unhappy time for most industrial organisations and Jack Sangster only just succeeded in keeping the company afloat in the financial sense, and in so doing changed the name to Ariel Motors (J.S.) Ltd. The only other models to be produced of noteworthy attention during the pre-war period were the Red Hunter range. These single-cylinder models were gradually developed over the next few years along with the Ariel Square Four. It was a hard time for all those involved in the motor cycle industry, but harder times lay ahead.

Soon after the war, in 1947, Ariel lost the services of Jack Sangster and in the same year merged with B.S.A., but as with the motor industry, machines continued to emerge from the factory with the name of the defunct company, in this case Ariel. 500cc and 650cc vertical twins were made in the late forties and early fifties and in the late fifties a 250cc parallel two-stroke twin-cylinder machine called the Leader was put into production.

In 1962 the Pixie 50cc single-cylinder machine was made to compete with the European and Oriental products, but never found success. However among motor cycle lovers everywhere the name of Ariel has succeeded over the years in earning respect and affection. The end came with a 50cc three-wheel moped which was discontinued shortly before the collapse of the B.S.A. empire.

4 ASCOT PULLIN

Cyril Pullin was renowned in the 1920s for his unorthodox but interesting motor cycle design. Between 1920 and 1925 he designed and helped produce the 'Pullin Groom' motor cycle with a scooter-like appearance and this was followed in about 1928 by the 'Ascot Pullin', which in its time was considered one of the most advanced machines made in England.

It should be clearly established that there was no connection between the Ascot Pullin and the Ascot motor cycle produced by the Ascot Motor Co. in about 1905 and 1906, which used Minerva or Antoine engines.

The Ascot Pullin was thought by most enthusiasts to be ahead of its time and a glance at its many attributes will be sufficient to convince most present day motor cyclists. On the mechanical side the Ascot Pullin had a magnificent 500cc o.h.v. engine gearbox unit horizontally mounted in a frame of pressed steel, which also found room for a large four-gallon petrol tank. The wheels were so designed that not only could they be removed easily in the event of damage or even a puncture, which was the everyday curse of the motor cyclist even in the twenties, but these could also be interchanged one with the other. To assist the rider, an instrument panel was fitted to the handlebars and for his greater comfort, apart from leg shields, a retractable windscreen was attached complete with a wiper. The passenger's comfort was provided for by a seat and foot-rests and all was included as standard equipment although the purchaser was certainly expected to pay one way or another for what he received. Unhappily the machine did not steer as well as a good motor cycle should. While they could be said to be getting good value for money the normal retail price of close on £80 was considered too high by the majority of motor cyclists, with the result that less luxurious machines that had better steering sold in preference to the Ascot Pullin. The present-day reader may well consider that the motor cycle described provided no more than present day standard equipment, which is a classic example of what are considered luxuries by one generation becoming necessities for the next. Unfortunately for Cyril Pullin, the time was not right for the provision of a luxury motor cycle at a luxury price and like so many other makes the Ascot Pullin had left the motor cycle scene by 1930.

5 BAT

The popular belief is that Bat motor cycles were so called because the manufacturer claimed his machine to be 'best after tests': B.A.T. Whether this was to be construed as a not too modest claim that his machines were better than his rivals or that his own machines improved their performance after testing has never been made clear. Actually it is an abbreviation of Batson, founder of the company in 1902. For the short duration of the Bat life, the motor cycles bearing this name (and claim) certainly made an impact on the motor cycling scene. The Bat was made at a factory at Penge in South East London, and the first machine saw the light of day in 1902. From the earliest days they were fitted with spring frames making for a more comfortable ride and better road holding. These early spring frames consisted of a small sub-frame carrying saddle and foot-rests suspended by springs from the main frame. Bat forks were of bottom link design with a pivoted and coil spring-supported U-shaped arm to carry the front wheel spindle anticipating Greeves by half a century.

T. H. Tessier took over the company in about 1904 and he proudly rode a Bat in the first ever Isle of Man T.T. race in 1907. From the very first, Bat dispensed with pedalling gear, claiming that the J.A.P. engine would see its rider safely up the steepest hills, a rare boast indeed in the first few years of the twentieth century.

Later Bats were generally 650cc, 770cc, 964cc and 980cc V-twin-cylinder machines (single-cylinder machines were dropped after 1912). Having entered the first T.T. race in the Isle of Man, Bats were entered in all but one of the pre-First World War T.T. races and, in the 1908 twin-cylinder class, took second place with W. H. Bashall in the saddle, who also recorded the fastest average lap speed of 42·25 miles per hour. Bats were fast and in 1910 the speed set up by H. Bowen in recording the fastest lap of 53·15 m.p.h. contributed to the change of course in the Isle of Man T.T. races. In 1911 the Mountain Circuit was first used for the Senior and Junior classes of the T.T. races. Bowen's lap speed had been regarded as far too dangerous for the short course and safety-conscious officials decided that a change of course would prevent serious accidents. However, fast though they were, another feature of the Bat racing performance was unreliability and more often than not Bat entries retired from the races they entered.

In their short post-war period of production, Bat took over the firm of Martinsyde in 1923 and for the last three years the motor cycle manufactured was sold under the name of Bat-Martinsyde. The company like so many others fell foul of financial troubles caused by increased costs of production and the competition from the newly available cheap, light motor cars and in 1926 the Bat motor cycle company ceased production. Batson's original firm had switched to the manufacture of office equipment in 1902 and duly celebrated its diamond jubilee in 1962.

6 B.M.W.

The Bayerische Motoren Werke, the Bavarian Motor Works, standing in Munich, Germany, represents all that is best in engineering. Founded in 1916, the company has successfully built quality engines for aircraft, motor cycles and motor cars and rightly has an international reputation for such work. The motor cycle was not a serious proposition at B.M.W. until the early 1920s when the first experiments with motor cycles were made. B.M.W. engines were prepared initially for motor cycles made by rival companies and the company did not manufacture their own motor cycle before 1923. The man responsible for this machine was chief engineer Max Friz. From the beginning Friz implemented his own ideas for a better motor cycle. His ideas, like Bradshawe's for A.B.C., allowed the horizontally opposed 500cc twin-cylinder air-cooled engine to be mounted well to the front of the frame and across it, and the engine power was conveyed through clutch and gearbox to a propeller shaft final drive. Shaft drive remained a feature of all future B.M.W. models. Since the first 500cc model came through the factory doors, B.M.W. have generally been associated with big twin-cylinder motor cycles, but apart from these B.M.W. did in the course of time make some single-cylinder motor cycles of between 200cc and 400cc engines with overhead valves. But it has to be admitted that the B.M.W. reputation was certainly earned by the 750cc twin-cylinder with world record breaking speeds, later continued with the 500cc supercharged models. As early as 1929 when the dust covers were hardly off the prototype B.M.W. motor car (an immaculate little limousine), Ernst Henne rode his 740cc twin-cylinder B.M.W. to a world record speed of 100·58 m.p.h. for a standing start mile on an autobahn adjacent to Munich in an incredible 35·79 seconds. Over the following decade, B.M.W. with Henne in the saddle won and lost the world speed records time and time again. Each new record seemed to stretch the machine to its maximum, only for it to be modified to attain even better performances. By 1932 Henne on B.M.W. also held the world record for the 'flying kilo' which means that the machine is already travelling at speed when the timing of the kilometre distance is commenced. The speed attained was 151·86 miles per hour. For his next attempt on the world speed record Henne was given a 500cc supercharged model. It must have been quite a sight for those few spectators scattered in vantage points near the Frankfurt Autobahn (Frankfurt motorway or freeway) when Henne's machine – totally encased with aluminium sheeting to aid streamlining – sped past like a bullet, in both senses, at a record breaking 169·4 miles per hour. The following year Henne improved his performance as he had to, in order to regain the world record lost during those twelve months, with a staggering 174 miles per hour. Speed records were not enough for B.M.W. and in 1937 machines were first entered for the prestige road race, the Isle of Man T.T. in the Senior event. For two years performances were good but not good enough for B.M.W. or indeed the Fuhrer who decreed that the 1939 Senior T.T. should be won by B.M.W. to show the world the superiority of all things German, not least their engineering prowess. There were not many in the motor cycling world of Europe who doubted the superiority of B.M.W. super-charged 500cc motor cycles even if they did not accept Hitler's other boasts. The sixth position in the 1937 T.T. race and the gallant fifth place in the 1938 event had been a little deceptive to all the uninitiated but it was no great surprise to the motor cycling fraternity around the world when Georg Meier on his B.M.W. led the field from start to finish of the 1939 race. His nearest rival, over a minute behind at the end of the race, did not greatly trouble him as it was works team-mate Jock West. The only event to mar the occasion for B.M.W. was the sad death of the third member of the team, Gall, who crashed in practice. The works machines showed many of the standard features of the machine which could be readily purchased by the man with the necessary money, such as the highly developed telescopic coil-sprung and oil-damped front forks which had been standard equipment on B.M.W.s for the previous three years. The finishing victory flag in the 1939 T.T. acted to all appearances as the starting flag to the next major event in Europe, the Second World War. Naturally enough B.M.W. provided motor cycles for the German troops and other machines for the military including aircraft engines and motor cars during the next six years. As far as the motor cycle side of the business was concerned, peacetime limits were imposed by the Allies after the war and in common with all German motor cycle manufacturers B.M.W. made motor cycles of the obligatory 250cc or less. The B.M.W. 250cc single-cylinder looked re-markably as though the company had merely divided an old 500cc twin to make two machines. All parts were suitably reduced versions of the former big model. In time the limit was raised, and B.M.W. resumed manufacture of the 500cc, 600cc and later 750cc models. In the racing world from the mid-fifties B.M.W. specialised in motor cycle sidecar events monopolising the Isle of Man T.T. races for many years and European Grands Prix events as well. With so many victories to their crdit in sidecar events it would not be right to pick out any particular race for comment, but mention must be made of a few of the most successful riders like W. Schneider, F. Camathias, F. Hillebrand, M. Deubel and F. Scheidegger not excluding the British rider Pip Harris.

The B.M.W. factory continues in production and the record book for this company at least cannot yet be closed. With their history and engineering experience many more wonderful B.M.W. achievements can be confidently awaited.

7 BROUGH SUPERIOR

George, the son of William Brough, was born in 1890 and from early childhood took an active interest in his father's activities in the development design and manufacture of motor cars and motor cycles. The first motor cycle that could be truly credited solely to William Brough was in 1902, and at the age of 16 George rode one of his father's machines in the A.C.C. End to End (John O'Groats to Lands End) trial along with his elder brother William junior. Whilst William junior took home a gold medal, George merely had the spiritual satisfaction of having taken part and the physical dissatisfaction of having pedalled his way round most of the course arriving at the finish three days after the last competitor. William Brough's success in motor cycle design and manufacture is illustrated in the achievement of entering seven machines in the London to Edinburgh trial in 1920 and taking home seven medals: six gold and one silver.

George went into partnership with his father, but their aims were different. George Brough, who wanted and intended to make a luxurious machine 'superior' to the average motor cycle, parted company with his father and started manufacture of the first Brough Superiors in Nottingham in 1919. The Mark I was driven by the huge 8 horsepower J. A. Prestwich engine. This V-twin overhead valve engine was known as the '90 Bore' (90 × 76 mm bore and stroke). The luxury included heavy plating to prevent rust and special exhaust and silencer design that became a hallmark of a Brough Superior, a muted monster indeed! Another distinctive feature of the Brough Superior throughout its years of manufacture was the bulbous nose tank which contrasted sharply with the angular box shapes appearing on nearly all other makes and it gave the Brough Superiors a smooth streamlined appearance. For these machines with sidecars, an alternative side valve engine was available. The Torpedo sidecar, looking like a miniature R100, was designed to accompany the Brough. The Brough Superior was also superior in price to the average motor cycle and good value though it was thought to be, the motor cycle was not in the price range of the average enthusiast, who had to be content with the advertisements, the records of its achievements, the shop window display and of course in due time the annual view at the motor cycle shows. The Mark II was given the long stroke Motosacoche 748cc engine. The reason for the quiet running of the Brough Superior apart from the exhaust and silencer system was the partial elimination of the usual noise caused by poppet valves and tappets. By 1920 the Brough Superior was already held in high esteem by the lucky owners.

One such owner wrote in eulogistic terms describing the Brough Superior as 'the Rolls Royce of motor cycles' and the letter being published, the phrase thereafter stuck. George Brough was not only responsible for design but also gave his machines the best and only true advertisements by riding them to success. In those days reliability was not a feature of every motor cycle and therefore a purchaser placed greater value on the achievements of machines in endurance trials than in short-term races, where on a given day, for a short time, a machine might just hold together. George Brough took gold medals in the 1920–2 Lands End trials and during his career he won over 200 awards, both in trials and races for he was no mean performer in either field. On his first appearance at Brooklands riding his original SS80 nicknamed 'Spit and Polish' by those who sneered at its well-kept appearance, he won the 1922 Experts scratch race lapping at 100 m.p.h. being the first to achieve this lap speed. Subsequently he won 51 out of 52 consecutive races in the years 1922 to 1923 on 'Old Bill' and in the fifty-second the machine won without him! Leading with only forty yards to go to the finish, a tyre burst on the front wheel causing the rider to fall but the machine continued to finish. The suggestion that 'Old Bill' should be given the trophy was hotly and successfully disputed by the rider who came second but finished still on his bike!

By 1924 the SS100 with overhead valve J.A.P. engine had been developed and was advertised with a guarantee that every machine had been timed over a quarter of a mile at a speed in excess of 100 m.p.h. George Brough had concentrated on the big 1000cc machines and was turning out for public purchase at this period only two models costing between £150 and £170 according to accessories and modifications. A short while later came the Alpine Grand Sports and as the name implies, intended for the sportsman. George himself won the Mount Cenis Hill Climb on the A.G.S. and to his horror upon returning triumphantly to Britain with the trophy found that the Customs men expected him to pay duty on it! The Alpine was followed by the similar Pendine. By 1927 a 750cc side machine was being manufactured, which apart from the standard quiet running expected of Broughs was economical on petrol doing about 80 miles to the gallon. 1927 and 1928 saw two different four-cylinder models at the annual motor cycle show in London with the innovation of the Draper spring frame for greater comfort. In 1929 the Black Alpine 680 (with hand change gear) was brought out and enthusiastically described as being able to 'glide along in almost perfect silence'. One could not always anticipate smooth roads and the 'castle' front forks were a godsend for shock absorbing. These were the result of experiments by George Brough and Harold Karslake whose combined design of a parallel tube with bottom link action was patented and put into production under the name of 'Castle' – naturally derived from Nottingham Castle. Two versions of Castle forks were used, long and short, on most models from 1925 until they were replaced by Monarch for the heavier machines in the mid-thirties. 1931 saw the development of the 'baby' Brough, a 500cc o.h.v. twin which was open to modification for racing purposes and on the market at 100 guineas. In 1933 came the development of the larger Broughs. The 11/50 of 1096cc could cruise with a sidecar at 75 m.p.h. but was still economical on petrol at 60 miles to the gallon.

After the death of his father, George returned to the original works of his father in Basford and from 1935 to the beginning of the war he continued manufacture there. A variation in 1935 was the adoption of 1000cc engines made by A.M.C. of Kent. By 1936 George turned his attention to developing the sidecar. He adapted the Austrian Felbers innovation of a loop frame sidecar, which required no cross-bracing and the body was therefore slung low and sprung on horizontal long semi-elliptical laminated springs, which gave the passenger extra comfort.

All men have dreams, but not all realise them. George devised his 'dream' motor cycle with considerable aid from F. Dixon and H. S. Hatch (well respected figures in the motor cycle world) and turned out the 997cc machine the 'Golden Dream', which incorporated all his ideals and was in fact the last design of Brough Superior. The proposed purchase price was £250, but unfortunately the model never went into general production. The war came and George Brough turned his attention to assisting his country in the best way he knew how. He designed a sidecar which could be adapted for machine-gun mountings or a fire-fighting unit, but the powers-that-be refused it. So his immediate attention went to the manufacture of precision components for aircraft, which were gratefully accepted.

Among the notable achievements of the Brough Superior were the Brooklands lap record speeds of 106·6 m.p.h. with sidecar recorded in 1937 and 124·51 solo in 1939. Both of these records were obtained by Noel Pope. Pope later attempted the world record on two wheels at Bonneville Salt Lake in Utah, USA in 1949, but whilst doing 150 m.p.h. he suffered a fall which left him comparatively unhurt but deterred his efforts. The Brough Superior had held the world record in 1937 when Eric Fernihough clocked 169·781 miles per hour. More recently in the late 1950s and early 1960s

'Bob' Berry made attempts on the world record lying prone on his stream-lined Brough Superior but once again a fall led to failure.

One of the more celebrated Brough Superior enthusiasts was T. E. Lawrence who between 1922 and 1935 owned one SS80 and six S.S. 100s, averaging about 27,000 miles *per annum* on them. He described his Brough Superior as 'reliable and fast as Express trains and the greatest fun in the world to drive' and in his last book *The Mint* the description of a ride on 'Boanerges' his Brough Superior at the time conjures up a word picture of the excitement and pleasure of riding. He unhappily met his death riding his Brough when swerving to avoid a cyclist who suddenly pulled out in front of him.

From 1940 the factory continued as precision engineers, but no more Brough Superiors were made and the machines that remain are jealously cared for by their owners who recognise the worth of the gentle giants.

8 B.S.A.

Many people wonder why it is that one of Britain's foremost motor cycle manufacturers appear to pass themselves off as gunsmiths. At first sight it would seem that the Birmingham Small Arms Company should be a case for prosecution under the Trade Descriptions Act! In fact the motor cycle company was derived from a group of gun makers originally called Birmingham Small Arms Trade Association from the late seventeenth century until the B.S.A. Company was formed in 1861.

Until about 1880 the company continued solely to make weapons, but then branched out into the world of manufacturing cycles. The story is told that a man named Otto presented the directors of the company with his own invention, a bicycle whose merits he proceeded to prove by riding it up and down the boardroom table! Needless to say the directors could not resist such a proposition and immediately ordered two hundred to be made. Cycles continued to be made and some tentative steps were taken in the direction of attaching the new-fangled internal combustion engine to effect their propulsion, but the Boer War once more took the attention of the company whose original interests after all lay in the making of war weapons.

With the turn of the century the B.S.A. Co., once more turned its attention to the production of parts for motor cycles manufactured else-where. It was not until 1910 that the first complete B.S.A. motor cycle took to the road. This was a $3\frac{1}{2}$ horsepower single speed model with cantilever front fork which was sold at a price of £50. An optional extra was a patent cone clutch in the rear hub called the 'free engine hub'. Early B.S.A.

designers paid particular attention to transmission, for example in 1913 the B.S.A. clutch was a three plate job operated by a toe and heel pedal. To start the engine the bottom gear was engaged and clutch freed, the latter being subsequently engaged to take up the drive. Gear changing was done on the valve lifter. It was fitted to machines during the First World War and continued until about 1920.

In the 1920s B.S.A. produced the side valve and overhead valve 350cc models and then the two speed 250cc side valve round tank model. This latter was not only cheap to buy, costing less than £40 it was also economic to run and an enjoyable ride. It was this model which was ordered by the G.P.O. when they inaugurated the telegram delivery service in Great Britain in 1924.

Nortons were not the only manufacturers intent on capturing the public eye with spectacular achievements of endurance and reliability during this decade. In 1924 a young trials rider, H. S. Perrey, led a team of four B.S.A.s on a mountain climb up Snowdon and got there in under twenty-five minutes! The achievement was subsequently emulated by many others but B.S.A. had been first. In about 1926 two men rode B.S.A.s on a round the world trip passing through some 24 countries in a matter of 18 months. Like Nortons the company had a machine built of spare parts gathered from a large number of dealers throughout Great Britain, which started first kick and went on to tackle a trial successfully. Perhaps the trouble with modern cycles is that they are built from parts coming only from one part of the country; certainly it is hard to find a machine nowadays that starts first kick!

B.S.A. were proud, and justly proud, of their Sloper (so called because of its sloping cylinder) which was built from about 1927 which quite by chance introduced the now world famous B.S.A. 'star' series. Some Slopers had special cams fitted and a high compression piston and to distinguish them from the standard model a red star was stuck conspicuously on them. Subsequently the Blue Star, Empire Star and Gold Star followed them off the factory floor.

From the earliest days B.S.A.s have been used by the Post Office for telegraph boys and deliveries and the small all red lightweight machines have up until recently been in constant use in the communication business.

Apart from the Post Office and many large companies, which have utilised fleets of B.S.A. machines on the basis of their consistent high performance and reliability, the army too has used them in large numbers. But the army naturally expected more from the company than motor cycles when the Second World War started in earnest.

By the 1950s B.S.A. were probably Britain's largest motor cycle manufacturers. In 1953 the company accepted the fact that motor cycles were not just a fanciful sideline and for the first time created a separate division called B.S.A. Motor Cycles Ltd. The B.S.A. Bantam, the 125cc model, was perhaps the most popular small motor cycle of the 1950s, a role now taken over by the Japanese machines such as Honda and Suzuki. With the 1960s the factory turned its attention more to the manufacture of the big engine machines like the Victor, a 441cc brought out in 1965, and the Rocket 3, a 750cc, three-cylinder machine introduced in 1968. The latter had the proud achievement of breaking nine American speed and endurance records in double quick time, and achieving a victory for Dick Mann in the Daytona race of 1971 at a record average speed of 104·7 m.p.h. In fact it was not until the 1950s that the company had either any real interest or success in International racing events. Prior to this there had been notable successes in trials, but nothing spectacular when speed rather than endurance or reliability had been the criterion for success. But in the 50's there were victories in the T.T. Clubman's races and many victories in International moto-cross events and a quite remarkable success at Daytona, Florida, in the USA when they once took the first five places.

As with all motor cycle manufacturers financial problems have forced changes at B.S.A. In 1971 the B.S.A. plant at Small Heath, Birmingham, transferred production to the Triumph factory at Meridan. B.S.A. continued under its own name with the Rocket 3, the Lightning and the Thunderbolt (single and twin carburettor versions of the 650cc twin-cylinder models).

Production of B.S.A. motor cycles in quantity ceased at the end of 1971 and apart from a small number of moto-cross machines no further motor cycles have been built at the B.S.A. factory since that time. This does not mean that the B.S.A. factory became derelict. In fact following the re-organisation and concentration of activity into the three big blocks of buildings at the front of the factory area, they became busier than ever. They continued as principal suppliers in the manufacture of parts and the complete manufacture of the three-cylinder engine, and in addition, have done much sub-contracted engineering work for big companies like British Leyland and Massey Ferguson.

In 1973 the B.S.A. group was taken over by Norton Villiers who formed Norton Villiers Triumph Ltd.

9 CALTHORPE

Like many other manufacturers Calthorpe initially utilised the engines of others in the motor cycles they offered to the public, and again like so many others the J.A.P. (or J.A. Prestwich) engine was one of the main engines so used. Calthorpes first came on the market in about 1910 or 1911 made by the Minstrel and Rea Cycle Company in the Midlands of England and the company name did not change to Calthorpe until just after the First World War. J.A.P. and Precision engines were used in their lightweight side valve single-cylinder machines and by the end of the decade the 147cc Aza was produced. By the mid-twenties they had introduced a new overhead valve 348cc model in which both pushrods were enclosed in a single tube, but by then the machines were being powered by their own Calthorpe engines. Towards the end of the twenties the Calthorpe image was changed with a re-design of its physical appearance. The main change was to put a white saddle tank and white mudguards on the machine to catch the public eye when so many other manufacturers were endeavouring to do the same with chromium plating. The new range of models was called the 'Ivory Calthorpe' and despite subsequent modifications this range continued until the end of Calthorpe production with the accent being placed on the manufacture of the 250cc, 350cc and 500cc o.h.v.s.

However, like so many other British manufacturers, the Second World War effectively brought Calthorpe's life to an end. Just prior to the war the Birmingham-based factory was bought out by Bruce Douglas of Bristol when the firm went into liquidation in 1938, but his plans for Calthorpe motor cycles never had time to see the light of day.

10 CHATER-LEA

At the turn of the century the Chater-Lea company was founded for the manufacture and sale of pedal cycle components. With the increasing interest in the newly developed motor cycle the company started to make frames and other parts for motor cycles, and during those early years experimented with clip-on engines attached to ordinary pedal cycles. But it was not until about 1908 or 1909 that the first Chater-Lea motor cycle, a V-twin cylinder machine, was available for purchase. Like all those to follow up until the First World War, this machine was fairly heavy and of rather robust construction. Chater-Lea did not make their own engines and a multitude of foreign-made products were tried in the early years including the famous Antoine, de Dion Bouton, Minerva and Peugeot, but the company favoured in time the British-made J.A.P. and Blackburne engines. The early Chater-Lea motor cycles were particularly popular for sidecar work, usually powered by J.A.P. V-twin engines of 770cc or 1000cc. The company was at the forefront (not unnaturally in view of their basic interest and knowledge in cycle components) in the development of spring forks, and were fitting them on their motor cycles as early as 1910. Another advanced feature of the Chater-Lea was the dropped top tube of the frame, sloping at the rear until it merged neatly with the saddle tube, making for a lower centre of gravity and greater stability of the machine. This concept was maintained by Chater-Lea designers and was further developed and improved upon during the twenties. One other notable development of the Chater-Lea Company in the first decade of the century was the introduction and subsequent production of a cycle-car. Three-wheel cycle-cars were very popular in those early days of motoring, before Henry Ford made cheap motor cars available to the public.

For 1913 the company only marketed the big twin cylinder 8 horsepower machine, but this featured their own remarkably advanced three-speed gearbox. In the following year, the same model was again available together with a 2¼ horsepower single-cylinder model. War, however, brought production to an end.

Before the war, Chater-Lea's racing success had been rather limited. Sixth place in the 1908 Single Cylinder event in the Isle of Man T.T. races had been achieved but that was to be the beginning and the end of their success in the T.T., retiring on every other occasion an entry was made. However, after the war the Chater-Lea company found considerable success on the race track, particularly in the hands of Dougal Marchant and Ben Bickell. A change in emphasis took place on the factory floor, where, after a brief resumption with the 1914 models, the company concentrated on the production of medium-weight machines fitted chiefly with Blackburne engines while at the same time making and developing their own engine. On the race track Dougal Marchant gained a considerable reputation, being both tuner and racer for Chater-Lea, and nowhere was he more feared by rivals than at the famous Brooklands track, the home of British track racing. In 1923 he won the 200-mile 350cc sidecar race at an average of 57·63 m.p.h., and repeated this success the following year when he also broke the world record for the 'flying' kilometre at 100·81 m.p.h. on a solo machine, which was the first time a 350cc motor cycle had exceeded 100 m.p.h. Unfortunately this did not rank as a world record since it was achieved by riding only in one direction. However, Marchant made up for this in 1926 when he took the world record for the 'flying' kilo for both 350cc and 500cc at 102·99 m.p.h. on his 350cc Chater-Lea with its extensively modified pushrod operated overhead valve Blackburne engine. During the mid-twenties Marchant also developed the 348cc overhead camshaft engine with face cam with considerable success.

On the 'sales' front, Chater-Lea were trend-setters for saddle tanks, featuring them on the 1924 models. During the twenties and early thirties larger Blackburne side valve engines of 550cc were extensively used by Chater-Lea for their sidecar model which incidentally was one of the machines favoured by the Automobile Association for their patrols in Britain during that time. The company, which was basically a family concern, ceased production by 1933.

11 COTTON

In about 1913 a young law student called F. Willoughby Cotton took his hobby of motor cycling not only seriously, but also critically. He was not content with the accepted framework of the current motor cycle which had evolved from the pedal cycle. He realised the shortcomings of the normal unmechanical frame design, which was distorted to accommodate the engine, the tank, the gearbox and other components. He formulated his 'triangulating principle' which was the introduction of a frame on the principle of a triangle with the steering ahead braced scientifically to the rear spindle. His stated 'Principle of Design' was that every necessary tube should be straight and subjected only to compression or tension with full triangulation so that all stress was concentrated at the apex of each set of tubes.

The advantages of this new design were that the motor cycle was light in weight yet free from the previous constant risk of fracture in the frame. With its low centre of gravity the machine was more stable on the road and the rider himself was in a better riding position, the saddle being made lower than on most other machines.

Needing assistance in putting his idea into practice, Cotton turned to Levis who produced the desired construction and were enthusiastic to keep the rights for manufacturing their own machine based on Cotton principles. Taking this as a sign that he had a valuable asset and being in two minds about his career as a lawyer, Cotton decided to make a name in the motor cycling industry. To raise capital for his own factory he sold the rights of a new type of carburettor he had designed to an American firm. With this money he commenced operations in Gloucester after the end of the First World War, the home of Cotton ever since.

Never afraid to take chances, he entered three machines in the 1922 Junior T.T. in the Isle of Man only just over a year after production had started. One of the riders on that occasion was an unknown Irish boy of 18 years of age called Stanley Woods. Woods was given the chance of a ride after a letter arrived on Cotton's desk from Ireland in which it was stated with true Irish 'blarney' that young Stanley was a great admirer of the Cotton machine and had said he could win the T.T. if only he could ride that machine. His claim was justified the year after, when he averaged a speed of 55·73 beating the more famous A.J.S. and Douglas. In that first

T.T. opportunity Woods certainly started with a bang. Having lost a plug at the start and run back to collect it he managed to get into fourth position at the end of a couple of laps. When refilling with petrol the practice was to leave the engine running in case of difficulties in restarting. On this occasion petrol spilled on the engine and both machine and rider were immediately set alight. Nothing daunted, after extinguishing both himself and his machine Woods rode on to come in fifth. The career of the Cottons in the T.T. races was highly successful and in the 1926 Lightweight section, the 'Bobbins' (as they were nicknamed) took the first three places.

Up to the Second World War the engines utilised by Cotton included Blackburne, Villiers, J.A.P. Barr and Stroud sleeve valve, Bradshaw oil cooled and Sturmey Archer. At their peak in the late 1920s, the production of the Cotton decreased in the thirties and suffered greatly with the beginning of the Second World War. Cotton was forbidden to deal with his foreign customers and told to produce for the home market yet was given no specific order to fulfil. Factories do not exist on promises alone and after going into liquidation in 1940 a Government order for machines arrived on Cotton's desk! So production continued. With the end of the Second World War the need of the Government ceased, money became short and the factory ceased to function after producing a limited number of models, one of which was powered by the 500cc side valve J.A.P. twin.

In 1953 two men with an urge to go into the motor cycle production business, Monty Delaney and Pat Onions, turned to the Cotton factory and, with the encouragement of its founder, opened the Cotton doors for business once more. The obstacles facing them might have deterred two less enthusiastic or able men. From this time on the famous Cotton frame disappeared and the factory endeavoured to put a new face on the machine and compete with the big names again. The new men put the machines in for moto-cross and then road racing with success which was little publicised with the arrival of the Japanese machines on the scene. But eventually the fight for survival proved too great and in common with so many other motor cycle manufacturers they were forced to close down.

Never afraid to take a chance or 'have a go' Cotton certainly made his name in the motor cycle world and will always be remembered for his 'triangles'.

12 D.K.W.

D.K.W. is another European company who specialise successfully in the manufacture of the small lightweight motor cycle. In the German company's case, the very earliest motor cycles they produced were lightweights. Originally D.K.W. motor cycles were designed and manufactured in

Zschopau in Sachsen and then moved to Dusseldorf after the Second World War.

The first D.K.W. machine designed by Hugo Ruppe was in fact a bicycle with a 119cc engine attached over the rear wheel. This was in 1919. Small beginnings for the company which in the next two decades was to acquire the reputation of being the manufacturers of the greatest number of motor cycles in the world. D.K.W. mainly concentrated their attentions on two-stroke single-cylinder machines, with a few twin-cylinder jobs in the 100cc to 500cc range. The company revolutionised the two-stroke motor cycle industry in the thirties by their introduction of a separate cylinder to act as a charging pump. It was in about 1912 that D.K.W. utilised the so called 'loop scavenge system' devised by Dr. Schnuerle, a new system of induction. Briefly the top of the piston was flat (in contrast to other systems), the inlet ports were so angled into the cylinder walls as to direct the flow of mixture during the transfer stroke across the combustion chamber and away from the exhaust port so that it swept the exhaust gas out through the normal piston controlled port. This proved more efficient and generally more realiable than the usual deflector top piston and certainly gave greater power.

Successful factories like D.K.W. were actively encouraged by the new Germany of the 1930s and road racing success was helpful to create a good image. In the late thirties D.K.W. lightweight machines were not only one of the most popular in the world, but also one of the most successful. Significant proof of this is that the record average speed of 78·48 m.p.h. recorded by E. Kluge when winning the 1938 Lightweight T.T. event was not surpassed for twelve years by machines of that cubic capacity. Even the improved standard of engineering design hastened by war did not provide a better motor cycle engine or system than used on this D.K.W. The engine was a 250cc water cooled two-stroke engine of split single design with its third supercharging cylinder. This praise should be qualified as supercharging was prohibited in international racing after the war, and the poorer low octane petrol then available did not assist the ordinary racing machine to achieve the speeds it might otherwise have attained.

After the Second World War, with a change of premises to Dusseldorf, the factory maintained its policy of manufacturing lightweight two-stroke motor cycles up to 350cc. This of course was a sound policy as the demand for relatively cheap and economical transport was greater than ever before. The recovery of Europe from its post-war poverty and need of economical transport in the late fifties, hit D.K.W. as it did all European motor cycle factories and resulted in the merger of D.K.W. with Zeirad-Union A.G. in Nuernberg. It is interesting to note that the Zschopau factory, now in East Germany, became the home of M.Z. motor cycles.

The latter day fame of D.K.W. is therefore chiefly in the more modest market of mopeds and motor scooters although even there D.K.W. technology evolved the automatic gear change for its Manuhurin model ahead of its competitors. But the D.K.W. factory continues as it started in the manufacture of the lightweight two-stroke motor cycle for which it has always been justly famous.

13 DOUGLAS

In 1905 the Fairy motor cycle was created by Joseph Barter – the 'flat' twin which was to become the world famous Douglas of dispatch-rider fame in the First World War. This Bristol-based firm developed the horizontal opposed fore-aft unit in about 1907 and continued utilising this system until well into the 1930s. William Douglas met Barter when the Douglas foundry made castings for the Fairy engines. The early Douglas models had direct belt drive, but in 1910 a two-speed gearbox with a design based on the back gear of a lathe was added, with the control on top of the tank. This was referred to as the 'tram driver' due to the fact that the lever was actuated fore and aft with a knob not unlike the control used on London trams. The true charm of the early Douglas motor cycles was in their lightness and ease of starting which in the days before the clutch system was developed and accepted, was accomplished simply by sitting astride the machine and giving a slight 'paddle' to set the engine in motion. Traffic stoppages – less frequent in those days – were endured with the engine in neutral, before another slight paddle enabled bottom gear to be engaged and the rider was once more on his way. Another attribute of the pre-war Douglas was its speed, reflected in racing successes such as their overwhelming victory in the 1912 Junior T.T. taking first, second and fourth places. W. H. Bashall, the former Bat-man, took the chequered flag almost five minutes ahead of his team mate E. Kickham who at least had the satisfaction of recording the fastest lap speed in the race. The following year, the best Douglas could do was a second place in the Junior T.T. with W. F. Newsome in the saddle, following the surprise winner Hugh Mason on his N.U.T. with two other Douglas machines in the first nine places.

The next important event for Douglas was in the First World War where many thousand were commissioned for official use by dispatch riders and were said to have performed admirably. After hostilities ceased in 1919 many war-time Douglas motor cycles were re-conditioned and sold to a public hungry for transport, bridging the gap until civilian motor cycle production could once more get into its stride.

Between 1920 and 1930 Douglas motor cycles were once more a power in motor cycle competitions although in a wider range of events, such as road racing, speed trials, hill climbs and the new discovery, speedway. In reliability trials the Douglas team of C. H. King, V. C. King and Spencer were regular winners of manufacturers' team awards during the immediate post-war period. In the late twenties Vic Anstice won many honours for Douglas at sprint events and at the world-renowned Brooklands track.

Earlier Tom Sheard on the new 500cc overhead valve Douglas won the Senior T.T. (the only Manxman to do so) and this combined with Freddie Dixon's victory in the sidecar race made 1923 a memorable year in the Douglas history. Dixon's machine was fitted with a banking side-car of his own design which, prior to the race, had been considered an unsafe device by many officials. However Dixon convinced them of its road-worthiness and proved it with a wonderful win. Freddie Dixon continued his racing career with a third place in the Senior T.T., again on a Douglas, although he was dogged with retirements in further attempts at success on Douglas machines. He was obliged to wait until 1927 for a solo win in the T.T. races. Meanwhile in 1925, on a H.R.D. Douglas, he had another sidecar victory in the Isle of Man T.T. races with L. Parker driving the first combination home.

On the standard production scene 1925 was also the year of the new E.W. model, which retained a modified fore and aft flat twin engine of 350 cubic capacity but up-dated in concept with the gear change for the three-speed box operated through the petrol tank which had an attractive sloping line in contrast with the flat parallel one used for so many years. The famous Douglas silver with blue panels colour scheme was retained and the new model attracted much attention at the British motor cycle show, another attractive feature being its price of £45. Douglas endeavoured at all times to keep the purchase price of their machines reasonable and this added greatly to their popularity in the years between the two world wars. The E.W. was immediately popular and continued with modifications for several years. In the years prior to 1932 Douglas designers always helped (intentionally or otherwise) the purchasers of their machines to save on motor taxes. Before that year there were different rates for motor cycle taxation dependent on the weight of the machine regardless of the engine's cubic capacity, so the lightweight Douglas motor cycles were much appreciated by their owners for this reason if for no other! The tax disc for motor cycles up to 224 pounds in weight cost half the amount charged for the heavier machines, while a sidecar added an extra £1 to the bill. All the Douglas 350cc machines came into the cheaper taxation class and even the C.32 500cc Douglas equipped with dynamo lighting came within the lower limit.

In 1928 speedway racing made its debut in Great Britain and for the first couple of years Douglas motor cycles dominated the tracks. In particular the 500cc o.h.v. Douglas was immediately popular and adapted to speedway purposes because of the model's aptitude for broadsiding due to its low centre of gravity. In time Douglas was superseded for dirt-track racing by Rudge.

The early thirties were significant years for the firm after a change of management and name to Douglas Motors (1931) Ltd., and the introduction of a new Douglas concept in motor cycling design in 1934. The new model was called the Endeavour and had a 500cc horizontally opposed twin-unit construction installed across the frame, as opposed to the in-line unit previously so popular with the factory. The new design fortunately did not commit the fore-aft unit to the scrap yard, as the Endeavour was not the success anticipated. But the Endeavour was an important landmark in the life of Douglas. Apart from the different positioning of the power unit, the significant changes to note were the four-speed gearbox with a hand-change at a time when most manufacturers favoured foot-change; shaft drive to the rear wheel via a spiral bevel final drive; the back wheel itself was quickly detachable for emergency tyre repairs. The engine was made with light alloy cylinders with cast iron liners and valve seatings between the head and barrel. The whole engine was only twenty inches wide when most of its contemporaries were far wider. The single plate fly wheel clutch was so light it could be operated by the little finger. The engine was set in a duplex loop frame and the model was listed originally at £72.10.0. when it made its surprise debut at the British Motor Cycle show of 1934. Despite its many fascinating and original features, the Endeavour failed to hold its own and after a few years the company were obliged to offer brand new models at £25.10.0. in order to recoup some of their losses on this venture. A sad time in the Douglas history but fortunately the set-back did not cripple the company.

Throughout the experimental period the factory had continued production of the popular 350cc in-line model, and with the Second World War the factory again began to assist the forces. In the early fifties the demand for motor-scooters enabled Douglas to manufacture the Italian Vespa under licence which they continued to do until 1960. For the man who preferred a little more power the Mark 3 de Luxe was brought out in 1949. This 348cc push-rod overhead valve transverse twin-cylinder machine was listed by the makers as the fastest standard 350 in the world, capable of 82 m.p.h. Its unusual features included a separate camshaft for each cylinder, a four-speed unit construction gearbox and a reversion to former ideas with foot-change of gears and final drive by chain. The engine was set in a tubular duplex frame with torsion bars supporting the rear swinging forks. The new Douglas forks were worthy of special comment as they were of radiadraulic loading link design.

Douglas motor cycles ceased to be made in the middle fifties and with the continuing success of the Vespas, the company decided to handle the British sales of another Italian motor cycling concern, Gilera. Sadly for the many enthusiasts no more of the delightful flat twin Douglas are coming off the production line.

14 THE DREADNOUGHT

Of recent years many engineers interested in motor cycles have constructed specials or 'one-offs' to obtain a machine incorporating in the specification all items which they consider necessary for a bicycle to perform the task for which it is required.

The Dreadnought is one of the earliest and possibly one of the most famous examples, built in 1902/3 by the late Harold Karslake in the works founded by W. E. Brough (father of George Brough). The construction of the frame was a unique design housing an M.M.C. engine of 3 horse-power purchased second-hand, in good condition, for 25/- (£1.25). It was a larger engine than the average type fitted at that time and considered desirable to avoid the use of pedals. A low saddle position was arranged (to avoid the dreaded side-slip) and many novel devices were incorporated which enabled the builder to accomplish fame as a rider for several years.

The requirements were general purpose use, such as a holiday tour of North Devon and Cornwall during 1906, accomplished on a single-gear machine with $4\frac{1}{2}$ to 1 ratio; two years later he climbed Porlock Hill, but by this time an N.S.U. two-speed gear had been fitted. In 1909 Karslake took part in the M.C.C.'s London–Edinburgh–London trial, but lost his award by being early at the time check at York. Competing in the Lands End Trial the following year, he was unfortunate enough to break an engine shaft, and he retired the machine temporarily. By October 1911, it had covered some 70,000 miles, and so earned the distinction of being exhibited on the Bat stand at the Olympia Show in London later that year.

In 1923 and again in 1927, 'Oily' Karslake, as he was affectionately known (due possibly to his connection with Speedwell Oils) rode the machine again in the M.C.C. London–Edinburgh Trial, now some 400 miles in length and including some formidable hills for that time. In the 1927 event he climbed all except one, due to belt slip caused by passing through the water splash at the foot of the hill, but gained a second class award.

The Dreadnought had the distinction of carrying number 1 in the first Sunbeam Pioneer Run from London to Brighton in 1930, when it was ridden by George Brough, and again on the 25th occasion of this event in 1961, when the author was honoured to pilot it once again to Brighton.

Harold Karslake donated the machine to the Vintage Motor Cycle Club and it can be seen on display at the Coventry Museum.

15 EXCELSIOR

Messrs. Bayliss, Thomas and Slaughter, three gentlemen with a common interest in developing and manufacturing bicycles, combined talents to form Bayliss Thomas and Co., in 1874. From the outset the name Excelsior was chosen for their machines and the emblem was that 'banner with a Strange Device'. The factory was set up in Coventry in the Midlands of England, where in 1896 the company first experimented with motorising their bicycles. Excelsior were the first British motor bicycles on sale to the general public and for that reason alone can claim pride of place in the British history of motor cycling. The first Excelsior motor bicycles had surface carburettors, hot tube ignition and were naturally belt drive. As a publicity stunt the company offered free rides to spectators at the Crystal Palace Exhibition of 1896 and not unnaturally succeeded in attracting all the attention. The early Excelsiors were fitted with de Dion and M.M.C. engines. Looking at an advertisement for a 1902 Excelsior one can see the main improvements claimed and selling features for the machine were the automatic oil lubricator, the 'Bayliss' patent anti-vibratory socket, the 'Bayliss' patent rim pulley attachment and the 'Bayliss' exhaust valve lift. The standard machine was sold with a 24-inch frame and 28-inch wheels with '12-inch Clincher A-Won' tyres. A 'special' was also generally advertised 'suitable for riders of short stature' with small wheels and cranks. What modern-day manufacturer would be so considerate as to cater for such needs? The standard $2\frac{3}{4}$ horsepower model could be purchased in those days for about £45. It would have been on such a model as this that Harry Martin rode in the first M.C.C. (Motor Cycling Club) run to Brighton in 1902 in the company of other early motor cycling pioneers. A year later in less sedate fashion Harry Martin recorded the first mile in less than a minute on a motor cycle (59 4/5 seconds to be precise) at the Dublin Phoenix speed trials.

The company was renamed the Excelsior Motor Co. Ltd., in 1910. Another record for the history books was created in 1913 when the company was responsible for the biggest single-cylinder motor cycle ever in general production, the 800cc side valve motor. Prior to the First World War Excelsior had purchased frames, mudguards and other parts from another Midlands company R. Walker and Son. Reginald Walker was originally in business manufacturing clock and ships' instrument cases but decided to strike off at a tangent and make parts for motor cycles. In 1910 this aspect of the business was doing so well, that Reginald Walker and his motor cycling-enthusiast son Eric decided to market their own complete motor cycle, which was called the Monarch.

After the Great War the Walkers took over the Excelsior company but continued to manufacture motor cycles bearing that proud name and emblem. The plant moved to Birmingham to join the Walkers and the production of motor cycles continued alongside the production of instrument cases. The company tentatively entered the field of manufacturing light cars but ceased production by the mid-nineteen-twenties. Eric Walker was a racing enthusiast and actively encouraged the use of Excelsiors in the major road races. In the hands of people like Walter Handley, Ernie Nott, H. G. Tyrell-Smith, Syd Gleave and Charlie Dodson, Excelsiors had their share of road racing success, highlighted by the victories of Crabtree and Syd Gleave in the lightweight events of the T.T. races in 1929 and 1933. Eric Walker realised that in the racing world he could not expect to win much if he used exactly the same engines as his rivals. So the company developed a four-valve engine built for them by Blackburne for the 1933 race, and Syd Gleave's 'mechanical marvel' justified its name. The 'Marvel' was quickly superseded by the overhead camshaft 'Manxman' a similar overhead camshaft model that was easier to manufacture. The pushrod 250cc 'Norseman', 350cc 'Warrior' and 500cc models proved popular with the motor cycling public in the thirties seeking two-wheel transport at a modest price. In the early days of mopeds, known pre-war as auto-cycles, Excelsior introduced the 'Auto-byk' with a 98cc engine of their own manufacture during 1937.

The 1902 man of small stature would have been more than content with the 'Welbike' made by Excelsior for the Second World War parachute troops. This miniature motor cycle or scooter could be folded away and carried by the man when he dropped into enemy territory and thereafter ridden by him to his planned objective. This machine was developed for peacetime civilian use as the Brockhouse-built 'Corgi' using the 98cc Excelsior single-speed engine, the 'Spryt' and later the two-speed 'Goblin'. At the same time the 250cc parallel twin two-stroke Talisman was put into production and became popular. With the general trend towards small cc machines in the 1960s Excelsior concentrated their entire resources on production of motor cycle assembly kits for 98cc and 150cc two-stroke engine machines. Now the company makes Britax equipment and accessories for cars and motor cycles.

Bayliss, Thomas and Co. were the first but not the last to make motor cycles with the name Excelsior. The German Excelsior was made in Brandenburg-Howel between the years 1901 and 1906, and from 1927 to 1939 the British-made Excelsior sold in Germany under the name of

'Bayliss-Thomas'. The American Excelsior was made in Chicago, Illinois, between 1908 and 1931 by the well-known bicycle manufacturer Ignaz Schwinn, and from 1917 Schwinn took over production of the Henderson. The American trade name of Excelsior disappeared in 1924 to be replaced by 'Super-X'. Schwinn ceased production of motor cycles altogether in 1931 but continued to make pedal cycles.

16 FRANCIS-BARNETT

Gordon Francis, son of Graham Francis of Lea-Francis fame, combined talents with Arthur Barnett in 1919 to create a new lightweight motor cycle for which they felt there would be a great demand. In the post-war era economical transport was at a premium, and the new motor cycle was developed not only with motor cycle enthusiasts in mind, but also for citizens who had need of reasonably priced personal transport, but were inexperienced with machines. This is not to say that the early Francis-Barnett motor cycles were cheap to purchase, but neither was any form of motorised transport immediately after the war. The policy of motor cycles primarily intended for transport was maintained thereafter.

Gordon Francis and Arthur Barnett were in fact related by marriage. They started their business in Coventry in the Midland area of England, and by coincidence the first Francis-Barnett motor cycle was constructed in the same workshop as the first English motor cycle, the Bayliss-Thomas Excelsior. This was regarded as a good omen. The first 'Fanny Barnett' was a 292cc side valve J.A.P. engined machine with a two-speed Sturmey-Archer gearbox. Since it was being made for transportation rather than sporting purposes, there were valanced mudguards to prevent rainwater or mud splashing the rider, a pannier-holder fitted behind the bicycle-type saddle, footboards with toe-guards for further protection, and a cast-aluminium case housing the primary chain for the chain and belt drive. The petrol tank was painted an attractive red and black making the whole machine a pleasing sight to the prospective purchaser. He or she would only have had cause to hesitate when the price of £84 was mentioned. But the Francis-Barnett found its market and the following years saw modifications to the original and expansion in the range of machines available to the public.

Although not built for sporting purposes the standard model was by no means slow and the 350cc model could quite happily clock fifty miles per hour.

The high purchase price continued to be a problem with the ever-increasing costs of production, and at first seemed insoluble. Happily

Gordon Francis came up with a revolutionary plan which would give the buyer a cheaper but even better machine. The basis for the idea had been conceived during the First World War when he was in charge of motor cycle repairs in the Army. He had observed with alarm the frequency of motor cycle frame fractures and was able to try out his ideas for overcoming this problem when back in the Francis-Barnett workshop. In 1923 he evolved a system of six pairs of straight tubes and one pair specially formed which made up the framework of the motor cycle. In appearance the frame below the tank formed an inverted triangle, the triangular-shaped tank was held by a similarly formed set of tubes and the framework from saddle to rear wheel hub and down to the foot-rest formed yet another triangle. Even persons with elementary geometrical or engineering knowledge will appreciate how much stronger a machine so built will be.

The wheels of the new Francis-Barnett were on spindles which could be easily removed and the whole was driven by a 147cc Villiers two-stroke engine with flywheel magneto and Albion two-speed gearbox, with final belt drive. It could be dismantled and put together again quickly for the makers ensured simplicity by using only two different-sized nuts throughout. Light in weight, easy to strip and re-assemble (one test showed two men could put it together in 20 minutes) it was also light and easy on the pocket, and cost only £25. The reason for the low price was that less costs were incurred in the manufacture of the parts required. Everybody was satisfied with the new little Francis-Barnett which was claimed to be 'built like a bridge' because of its constructional principles. The frames were in fact under guarantee against breakage 'for ever'.

The 147cc was not the only machine to come out of the factory in 1923, as there were also 250cc and 350cc machines with sidecars available. But Francis-Barnetts' interests lay principally with the new 147cc machine which in the next few years was accompanied by a 172cc model. In one of the many tests carried out by enthusiasts in the 1920s, Mrs Meeten rode just over 1,000 miles in five days and averaged 196 miles per gallon. The whole journey cost her less than ten shillings (50 pence) in petrol and oil, a sad reminder of the cheap price of fuel in those by-gone days. Another stunt of the mid-nineteen-twenties was the ride up Mount Snowdon on motor cycles. The Francis-Barnett riders of 1926 were not the first, but were certainly among the speediest in climbing the 3,600 feet in about 22 minutes. A first was recorded in 1927 when Drew McQueen rode his Francis-Barnett 172cc machine up Ben Nevis in just over 2 hours. It was in that year that Francis-Barnett finally dropped the idea of belt drive, having offered the alternatives of chain or belt drive over several preceding years.

The next impact on the motor cycling scene made by Francis-Barnett was the Pullman, a 344cc vertical in-line twin with two-stroke Villiers engine. This became available to the public in 1928 and in the next two years Francis-Barnett followed the fashion which called for cream-coloured machines. The 250cc Cruiser brought out in 1933 typified the Francis-Barnett attitude to the traveller who did not want to dress up to keep clean on his or her motor cycle. This model was virtually wholly enclosed. The front mudguard enveloped the wheel as did the rear mudguard, casing enveloped the engine and leg shields protected the rider from outside sources of dirt. One could ride the Cruiser in full evening dress and arrive immaculate. Production of this model continued up until the Second World War as did the manufacture of the 'Stag' model, a 248cc Blackburn-engined machine with overhead valves first introduced in 1935.

The other major events of the pre-war period were the manufacture of a 125cc model called the Snipe and an even smaller machine, an autocycle called the 'Powerbike' with 98cc engine, both of which made a return immediately after the end of the war. These models and other two-stroke lightweights were to be the order of the day from that time and continued in production under the name of Francis-Barnett even when the company amalgamated with Associated Motor Cycles Ltd., the Matchless concern, in 1947. In the late fifties production was transferred to the Birmingham-based James Company workshops where they concentrated on making Villiers-engined two-stroke machines under 250cc. The firm, now under its new management, continued to make neat and economical motor cycles and mopeds until A.M.C. Ltd. ceased to operate.

17 GILERA

Guiseppe Gilera was the founder of a motor cycle company that in its heyday was to produce the most powerful engines and most successful racing machines in the world. Guiseppe Gilera's first love of motor cycles came as an enthusiastic young rider and with the aim of making better machines to ride, he started his own factory in 1909 in Milan, Italy. Gilera decided that the only way to improve the quality and performance of the motor cycles he rode would be by making his own engines and from the earliest days his motor cycles used only Gilera-built engines. From the beginning the 500cc was favoured by the young manufacturer and it is in this class that they hit the headlines over the years. The first 500cc models were side valve single-cylinder machines but as time passed and the Gilera became more popular, the range was extended to include 250cc and 600cc models.

It was perhaps not until the late thirties that Gilera came to world-wide attention with the famous 'Four' which took the racing scene by storm, and showed itself to be in a class on its own. This new engine was based on the former Rondine design by Carlo Giannini. The Rondine motor cycle had a fairly chequered career in the hands of its original manufacturers, the Compagnia Nazionale Aeronautica and subsequent owners, before all rights to its design were purchased by Gilera in 1936. The success of the Rondine four-cylinder machine in races had often been thwarted by difficulties in handling experienced by its riders and there was still room for improvement in the engine department. The remedy was swift. Within a couple of years the Gilera Four had made its racing name. It was a 500cc transverse four-cylinder machine, supercharged and water-cooled. The massive engine was held in the duplex cradle frame by webs at each end of the crankcase, and road holding and comfort was improved by the pivoting fork suspension controlled by horizontal units and massive friction dampers. Gilera could point to his first racing machine with pride, since it achieved the world speed record of 154 miles per hour and the world motor cycle speed record of 171 miles per hour. With modifications the same model won the 1939 Ulster Grand Prix at a record average speed of 97·85 miles per hour, with D. Serafini in the saddle. In the same year Gilera won the coveted European 500cc championship.

The greatest racing success was yet to come. In the post-war period Gilera further developed the four-cylinder machine for racing, at the same time manufacturing small single-cylinder overhead valve machines of 150cc and 250cc for public purchase. In 1950 the Dutch and Belgian Grands Prix were added to the list of Gilera 'Four' victories. The factory had not entered the Isle of Man T.T. races prior to the Second World War and their early attempts in the post-war period were thwarted by mechanical failure. But the warning was given by the fast pace set by machines which unhappily 'packed up' before the finish. Reg. Armstrong took third place in the 1953 Senior event and in the following year ace rider Geoff Duke improved that position by one. Duke had changed his allegiance to Gilera from the Norton team by this time and his former colleagues who reigned supreme in the early fifties could feel the hot breath of Gilera on the back of their racing necks. In the following year 1955, Gilera were in front. First and second place in the Senior event were easily taken by Duke and Armstrong, and Duke nearly became the first man to record an average lap speed of 100 m.p.h. when he turned in a speed of 99·97 m.p.h. That honour in fact fell to Bob McIntyre on another Gilera in 1957 when winning the Golden Jubilee Senior race with a fastest lap speed of 101·12 m.p.h. In the same year a 350cc Gilera also took first place in the Junior event, being ridden once again by Bob McIntyre. The difference in the fastest lap speeds between McIntyre's 350cc Gilera and John Surtees' winning 500cc M.V. Augusta in the Senior event the year before was a trivial 4/10 of a mile per hour. In 1957 McIntyre set an incredible 97·2 miles per hour 350cc lap record. Since those heady days when four-cylinder Gileras were the fastest on the racing circuit, other riders to record success on Gilera machines have been John Hartle and Phil Read. When writing of successful road race riders in the Gilera history it would be wrong to omit mention of earlier champions like Piero Taruffi who did so much for Gilera on the track and also assisted in developing early Gilera 'Fours' prior to the Second World War. An example of the quality of Gilera racers, both men and machines, was demonstrated by the exhibition ride of Geoff Duke in the Isle of Man in 1973. In the interval between the Manx Grands Prix races he rode a circuit of the course on a twelve-year-old Gilera racer and recorded an average of 87 m.p.h., which means speeds of over 100 m.p.h. in places. After such a long absence for both machine and rider, this average speed speaks volumes for their joint ability.

Like so many other European manufacturers the latter-day standard production Gileras have largely consisted of lightweight 98cc, 125cc and 175cc single-cylinder models. The racing successes of Gilera have added to the company's prestige, and the sound policy of manufacturing small single-cylinder machines has ensured survival when other equally successful racing motor cycle companies have been obliged to go into liquidation.

18 HARLEY-DAVIDSON

It is almost to be expected that a motor cycle made in the United States of America will acquire slogans eulogising the machine over a period of years, but the Harley-Davidson is perhaps the most famous motor cycle being manufactured in America today, certainly the one with the greatest history. How then did the 'silent gray fellows', 'the motor cycle magnificent', and even 'the bunch of dynamite' begin? The answer is in a Milwaukee basement workshop at the turn of the century when William Harley and Arthur Davidson, a draughtsman and patternmaker respectively, got together to experiment with mechanising a bicycle. They had met working in a motor cycle factory and with the spirit of adventure started their now famous venture. Arthur's brother Walter was called in to assist and he had the pleasure and privilege of road testing their first product, a 3 horsepower single-cylinder machine, and Walter in fact road-tested every new model for the next twenty-five years. Soon afterwards Arthur's oldest brother William joined the organisation making the firm a truly family organisation, which it continued to be through the years, one generation succeeded by the next, until 1969, when the company merged with American Machine and Foundry Co., and 'went public'.

As early as 1907 the police force started using the Harley-Davidson motor cycle as a means of official transport. In the USA the police force is divided into many departments within the various states, but in due time over three thousand departments were using the 'Harley' and for many people the Harley-Davidson became synonymous with the motor cycle cop!

Motor cycles did not catch on in the USA in quite the same way as in Europe and a good reason postulated is the fact that motor cars were very quickly on the scene and selling at remarkably low prices. In Europe there was also the attraction that the motor cycle would ride the road better and possibly be more reliable than the contemporary motor car. The average distance to be covered by the traveller in Britain would be less than for his American counterpart and for that reason alone a car would always prove more comfortable and convenient. Added to this was the unaccountable fact that the European was more enthusiastic about motor cycling as a sport or hobby than the men from across the Atlantic. Today the reverse may well be true.

For one reason or another in the early days of motor cycling the Harley-Davidson really only had one major rival in the USA, the Indian, which unhappily ceased production in 1959.

The early Harley-Davidsons were all high-power models with direct belt drive and twist throttle control. Bill Harley went off to university to get an engineering degree and returned to become the company's chief engineer. Early successes in 'endurance runs' (or trials as we would call them in Europe) did not cause complacency. Harley's aim was to produce a twin-cylinder model, which he achieved in about 1909. Features of the new Harleys were the now familiar low saddle position on a frame which had the front tube vertical and coil or magneto ignition. The wide wheels were to come at a much later date. Chain drive was incorporated about 1912.

Before the First World War found yet another use for the Harley-Davidson, throughout America the machines were being used by police, telephone companies and postal services. In the war the American military men found more use for motor cycles than did the British services. Not only were the Harleys 'conscripted' for construction battalions, the signal corps and medical corps, but also for transporting arms and ammunition. By this time they were known not only for their power and reliability, but also for their speed, having shown this in a hundred-mile test averaging 89 m.p.h. for the distance. Although they rarely sponsored their machines in races Harley-Davidson were able to capitalise on the enthusiasm of racing men with their slogan 'Don't blame us if a Harley-Davidson wins the race!' So when America entered the war it was not unnatural to see that the chosen motor cycle was the big Harley. Whether it was 'army surplus' or to remind the nation of the part they played in the war, Harleys for many years afterwards continued to be painted khaki!

Renewed enthusiasm for motor cycles after the war was encouragement enough for Messrs. Harley and all the Davidsons. The Big Twin model J was introduced to the eager public together with a sporting model which for the first time had a counterweighted crankshaft, enclosed timing gear drive to the generator ignition unit and new exhaust system, leading link forks for the front suspension, the typical foot-boards rather than foot-rests and 3-inch tyres. One of the little exercises undertaken in the early twenties was the Canada to Mexico run, which makes the Lands End to John O'Groats trial seem like a Sunday afternoon outing. On one occasion a Harley-Davidson clipped five hours off the record time for the 1,700 mile run.

Expansion was the main object in the 1920s whether of production or market. Harley-Davidson saw Europe as a prospective market and with that in mind introduced the comparatively small 350s into their production line, which picked up the nickname of the 'peashooter'. This appeared with the unusual bomb-shaped tank, 'hooded' mudguards and wide wheels. The British public at least were already aware of the existence of Harleys, having witnessed another Davidson (no relation to the firm) become the first man to lap Brooklands in excess of 100 m.p.h. in about 1919. The British manufacturers therefore were already on their guard for the prospective invasion. As can be seen elsewhere in this book British machines in the 1920s were more than a match for outside competitors. The 'Depression' also hit production in the Harley-Davidson factory with the result that the challenge never really materialised. The early thirties were a hard time for the company.

An innovation of the thirties was the now familiar 'balloon' tyres, 500×16 Firestones. Another new step was the production of a three-wheeler called a 'Servi-car'. This like the motor cycle was immediately utilised by the police forces of America and also became very popular with delivery services. In 1936 an attempt to open a factory overseas in Japan was not destined to be a success. Another war, another day for Harley's. Nearly 100,000 Harley-Davidson motor cycles were used in this 'world event'. The post-war needs were for economical motor cycling and manoeuvrability, which once again caused the company to bring out a smaller model, this time the 125cc two stroke which, like the B.S.A. Bantam, owed much to the conquered German D.K.W. design.

As mentioned previously, in the early days the directors rather frowned upon the racing fraternity. Over the years the attitude changed, as can be seen from the number of world records achieved by riders on Harley-Davidsons with assistance in some way from the company. For example, in the 1930s Petrali secured the world record with an astonishing average speed of 139·15 m.p.h. But the 'biscuit' was truly taken by the company when in the early 1950s a big Harley won a race over half a mile with a Mustang Aircraft – the latter was obliged then to take off!

The company ceased to be a family business in 1969, but by then they had already expanded into Europe taking over the Aer-Macchi factory in Verese, Italy. Business, as one would expect with anything to do with Harley-Davidson, continues to be big.

19 HENDERSON

William G. Henderson had the distinction of being responsible for two of the most celebrated makes in the history of motor cycling. In a life cut tragically short by a fatal accident in 1922 he was founder and designer of both the Henderson and the Ace four-cylinder motor cycles. In eleven short years Henderson inscribed two names on the motor cycle roll of honour.

Starting the Henderson Motor Cycle Company with his brother Tom in Detroit, Michigan, in the United States of America, William Henderson had his first motor cycle off the production line in 1912. The first model, like all succeeding Henderson motor cycles, was a four-cylinder machine with a distinctive and unusually long wheelbase close on 65 inches. Its original method of starting was by way of hand crank, rather similar to that used by most old cars, operated when the machine was up on its stand.

Henderson also finished all his machines in distinctive colours, the first models black with gold stripes, and red stripes on mudguards and tank panels, followed in subsequent models by a basic blue with gold stripes. Part of the reason for the lengthy wheel base was the positioning of the foot-board in front of the engine. Subsequent models were made with a shorter wheel base when two foot-boards were fitted outside the frame on either side of the machine.

The first Henderson seated the rider on the lengthy cylindrical tank just in front of the rear wheel, necessitating rather long handlebars for controlling the machine. Provision was made for possible passengers with a saddle on the tank in front of the driver. This meant that the passenger not only partially obscured his driver's vision of the hazards ahead, but also impeded the free movement of the handlebars and consequently the front wheel. However there were very few other criticisms and Henderson soon abandoned this position for passengers.

Other features of the first model were that it provided a remarkably smooth, quiet ride and a reliable performance. The 1912 model, like its successor in the following year, was single-speed only but this did not prevent a New Yorker, Carl Stevens, from riding one round the world, the first motor cyclist to perform this feat. In 1912 this 7 horsepower motor cycle could be purchased for a mere 325 dollars and it was worth every cent.

Henderson modified his motor cycle over the next few years. The wheel base was shortened, the riding position was lowered and improvements to the front forks all helped the machine's handling. The shape of the tank was altered and a two-speed gearbox was first introduced in 1914, to be replaced in 1917 by a three-speed version. The Henderson had quickly earned a reputation throughout the United States for reliability and proved its performance in endurance trials. One of the formidable tests was the Coast-to-Coast run across the USA over more than three thousand miles of rough terrain. In those early days the made-up road was confined to the cities and anyone who ventured beyond the city limits did so at his own risk. Motor vehicles found the going particularly hard and their drivers likewise. Allan Bedell, a Henderson enthusiast and a rider with a promising future, made a record-breaking run from Los Angeles to New York City in seven days and sixteen hours, to beat the previous best performance by nearly four days. Tragically that promising future was never realised for young Bedell was one of those who did not return from the First World War.

Another endurance record to fall to the 1917 Henderson was the Canada to Mexico run called the 'Three Flag Route'. Roy Artley on his Henderson Four broke the two-year-old record when riding the seventeen hundred miles in three days and twenty-five minutes. The Americans have always had a flair for publicity stunts – elsewhere in this book the early boasts of Edward Joel Pennington are described – but even he would have been proud to have originated the 'roller coaster run'. This daring feat was performed by one August E. Walter, better known as Blick Walter, who confidently rode his 1917 Henderson Four round a roller coaster track in a Californian fair ground. He presumably still holds the world record for this run!

Whether it was this last feat or the overall performance over a number of years Henderson was brought to the eye of its American rival Excelsior. In 1917 the Excelsior chief Ignaz Schwinn made the Henderson brothers 'an offer they couldn't refuse' and took control of the Henderson Motor Cycle Company in a deal which allowed the brothers themselves to continue work for a short while. The motor cycle produced under the new regime was the Excelsior-Henderson although it is more commonly known as the Henderson X because of the transfer on the petrol tank showing a large red X with the name 'Henderson' emblazoned across it in gold letters.

Both Henderson brothers severed their connection with the Excelsior-Henderson in 1919 and William G. Henderson decided to start again on his own this time without the able support of his brother Tom in a new motor cycle venture. He started his second business in Philadelphia making another four-cylinder motor cycle, this one to be called the Ace. Ace were only in production for three short years until Henderson's death, and the motor cycles manufactured by him were 1168cc and 1229cc air-cooled four-cylinder side valve machines. After Henderson's death the Ace factory was bought up by the Michigan Motor Corporation and later sold to Indian, hence the Indian-Ace produced in the late nineteen-twenties.

But with William Henderson's departure from the Excelsior-Henderson scene, the factory did not cease to thrive. New blood was injected into the design team in the person of Arthur Lemon. Lemon had been with Hendersons from 1915 and transferred with the company in 1917 to Schwinn's organisation. His new design for 1919, the Model K, was a dramatic change from the former Henderson models, with a larger engine and a new type of cylinder and was the first American motor cycle with full pressure lubrication to all bearings. This model was so popular that production of it continued until 1921, while the De Luxe model K continued to be made until 1929. The De Luxe had a guaranteed speed of 80 m.p.h. and an unusual feature, a reverse gear.

Lemon continued at the helm until the fatal accident to Henderson in 1922 caused him to join Ace to assist at their time of crisis. It was in that year that the great American rider Wells Bennett created one of his many records, taking the much-coveted twenty-four hour record previously held by Cannonball Baker on his Indian. Bennett, riding his Henderson X model K de Luxe said to be a standard model, covered 1562·54 miles in the twenty-four hours period and averaged over 65 m.p.h. This record stood for another fifteen years. If this highlighted the reliability of the Excelsior-Henderson K De-Luxe, then Fred Ludlow's 127·1 m.p.h. for the fastest quarter-mile in the world in 1924 proved that endurance was not obtained at the expense of speed. These two qualities always appeal to motor cyclists and to catch the faster men many police forces decided to ride the same machines. There is an American saying 'it takes a Henderson to catch a Henderson'!

Modifications of the De Luxe in the mid-twenties included a change of frame to one which sloped downwards at the rear and allowed for a lower saddle position and the addition of balloon tyres, always popular with American motor cyclists.

A. R. Constantine transferred from the rival Harley-Davidson to take over design of the Henderson X in about 1928. He aimed at a lower riding position and better engine performance and to this end he designed the K.J. model which upon its appearance and performance merited its nickname of the 'Streamline Henderson'. The modified version, the K.L., was reputed to go from a mere ten miles per hour to one hundred and ten miles per hour all in top gear.

During the twenties Henderson engines were also used to power light aircraft and turned in many remarkable performances. But the depression was hovering on the horizon and as it enveloped the country, so it naturally affected the sales of all motor vehicles. Schwinn realised that however good his products were, there would be little market for their sale in the foreseeable future and decided to close down the motor cycle manufacturing side of the business in 1931, while continuing the pedal cycle business. It was therefore no reflection upon the Henderson X as a motor cycle that no more were made after 1931. Happily there are still Henderson motor cycles in existence as constant reminders of their once great presence in the world market of motor cycles.

20 HONDA

The Honda Motor Company was established in 1948. By 1950 their motor cycle production was a mere 9 per cent of the Japanese market with no influence on the outside world. The early 1950s were dominated by the British machines which with years of pedigree behind them were correctly thought to be better, sounder and more reliable motor cycles. Complacency is a dangerous attitude. Soichiro Honda was not a man to shy away from what must have been an awe-inspiring challenge. Nortons, A.J.S., B.S.A., Velocette, and Triumph appeared to have a strangle-hold at least on the British market. By 1958 however Honda had increased output four times over and were looking for a way to catch the buyer's eye. The best advertisement was success in racing, and they scored their first success in the US Catalina Race in that year. 1959 saw the first Honda in the Isle of Man and in 1961 they took both the 125cc and 250cc world championships. Honda was making his impression especially in the low capacity field. His later policy was to make machines to satisfy the requirements of everybody everywhere and he had realised that the small, mobile, easy-to-start 50cc was the machine to meet such a need.

Previous attempts to produce a good 50cc by other manufacturers in most cases had met with conspicuous failure due to the unreliability of the finished product. Most British manufacturers refrained from even trying to make such an animal. Previously it had always been assumed that motor cyclists would only ride a machine that had to be kick-started, was prone to violent vibration during the ride and the introduction of 'gadgets' such as the electric starter, automatic clutch and even automatic transmission seemed unwanted gimmicks. In fact, of course, the motor cyclist is a man of many faces. There are enthusiasts who like nothing better than the machine in parts by the side of the road, or a hard ride in trial or racing conditions, but there is a market for the motor cyclist about town who is not averse to a few luxuries when riding two wheels. Honda, like Scott before him in 1908, introduced his 250cc twin with pistons moving in opposite directions to cut down vibration. The speeds of the small machines was and still is quite remarkable: for example, nearly 100 m.p.h. out of a 250cc. Remembering that second-hand cars could be easily purchased for the price of a new motor cycle, the attraction of two wheels had to be obvious enough to keep a market amongst people who merely wished to travel from home to work or on pleasure drives. Motor cycles had to be more economical to run, but comfort and reliability were the other attractions offered by Honda.

1961 was considered the turning point. Before then, if the man in the street was asked to name a motor cycle, one of the famous British or European makes would have sprung to his lips, but now inevitably the name would be Honda. Although popular in Europe and Asia, nearly a third of the sales were made in the USA. The enthusiasm of the founder is reflected in the attitude of his employees in the factories at Saitama, Hamamatsu and Suyuka. By 1961 these three factories alone were turning out over 3,500 motor cycles per day. Perhaps their success is not surprising. After confining himself initially to the small cc market (250 and less) Honda has now produced four-cylinder models of 350, 500 and 750cc to compete with the best in the world, both on the race track and in market sales. In racing circles the leading Honda exponent has been Mike Hailwood who has electrified spectators all round the world with performances and victories in probably every international race of consequence. Where others have fallen victims to financial problems, Honda's have prospered and the outlook for this Japanese organisation seems as bright as ever.

21 H.R.D.

It is not often that a celebrated racing motor cyclist turns successful manufacturer and in this respect Howard R. Davies was almost unique. Winning the Senior T.T. race is usually regarded as a wonderful achievement and perhaps the crowning glory of the racing motor cyclists' career, but when it was achieved in 1921 by Davies on a 350cc A.J.S. motor cycle in competition naturally with 500cc machines, it truly made history. Indeed Davies' victory should not have been allowed to stand strictly speaking as the tyre dimensions did not accord with those laid down for the Senior race machines, but fortunately sportsmanship counted for something in those days and overwhelmed the professional objections which could have spoilt this race. A further remarkable feature about this combined Davies and A.J.S. success was that the machine was driven by the same engine in the Senior race that had just been used (naturally under heavy stress) in the Junior race. This is a tribute to the A.J.S. reliability and stamina as well as its speed. Davies had in fact already picked up a second place in the Junior which an ill-timed puncture prevented him from winning. By 1921 Howard Davies had already built a good racing reputation with a second in the 1914 Senior T.T. on a Sunbeam to his credit. However subsequent big race success often eluded Davies, due not to lack of skill but to the unreliability of the machines he rode. With a view to changing this situation he decided that 'if you want a job well done, you do it yourself'. Together with the technical assistance of Massey of Massey-Arran fame, Davies went into motor cycle production in 1924 at his new works in Wolverhampton. Howard Davies believed that a rider was a considerable factor in slowing a motor cycle down in a race and therefore lowered the saddle while maintaining the relatively high position of the petrol tank, which was necessary if the long stroke engine was to remain vertical in the frame. He removed the usual impediment of a lower tank rail altogether. The tank itself with the proud gold letters H.R.D. emblazoned on the side was specially adapted by means of careful cutting away to overcome the difficulties created by the valve gear position and size.

The engine chosen to power this new motor cycle was the J.A.P., there being two models of 350cc (sports and racer) and two models of the 500cc (sports and sidecar).

The foot-rests with brake and auxiliary oil pump pedals were adjustable to meet the needs of the individual rider and the whole was set in a rigid cradle frame. Davies wanted a machine to win races as success was the best advertisement. Inevitably the T.T. races represented the big test for him, a way of proving that he had made worthwhile innovations in motor cycle manufacture and that he himself was a great rider of the present and not just the past. He was only a year into production and in competition with the great names in motor cycle manufacturing circles and the equally great names of their riders. Yet Howard Davies rode his own machine to victory in the 1925 Senior T.T. and beat a field that included the great Alec Bennet and Jimmy Simpson, and he took second place in the Junior. Sadly he was not to know personal success like that again, although an H.R.D. and Freddie Dixon won the 1927 Junior T.T.

The General Strike of 1926 greatly affected H.R.D. who like so many motor cycle manufacturers through the ages perpetually walked a financial tight-rope. The H.R.D. motor cycles were sold at 'luxury' prices while other motor cycle prices were becoming more realistic for the would-be purchaser.

H.R.D. went into voluntary liquidation in 1928 and were eventually put back into production by Philip Vincent under the new name 'Vincent-H.R.D.'

Under new management the Vincent-H.R.D. now manufactured at Stevenage showed very little physical resemblance to the H.R.D. which had formerly been on the market. The leading innovation to improve the motor cycle still selling partly under its old name was the Vincent spring frame. This gave the motor cycle an extra diagonal frame tube on each side of the bike running from steering head to a rear pivot supported by Timken taper roller bearings. Phil Vincent later changed the J.A.P. engines for either his own or Blackburne or Villiers.

Howard Davies apparently did not retain any control or have any say in matters after Vincent took over, despite the fact that his name continued to be used on the machine for selling purposes. At no time does it appear that Phil Vincent saw fit to consult with Howard Davies on any design feature or alteration and to all intents and purposes the motor cycles produced after 1928 had no connection with H.R.D. Davies himself reverted to his former occupation as a sales representative for motoring companies.

In 1937 Phil Vincent put his first 1,000cc Vincent H.R.D. with high camshafts into production and it is with these big bikes that Vincent's name will always be connected. It was not until 1950 that Vincent finally dropped the H.R.D. tag and continued production under the sole name of Vincent until 1956. History has a habit of repeating itself. Like the Howard Davies organisation before, Vincents finally succumbed to financial pressures and ceased to be produced. It was a strange quirk of fate that it was only after this that the two men Davies and Vincent should meet for the very first time. A year or so later Howard R. Davies died having contributed so substantially to both the manufacturing and racing history of motor cycles.

22 HUMBER

It was in 1868 that Thomas Humber, later to become one of the greatest names in the world of transport, started production of velocipedes at his workshops in Nottingham. Humber bicycles were of such quality that they were the choice of three generations of British monarchs and the company he established was responsible in the course of time for the production of motorised bicycles, tricycles, quadri-cycles, tricars, motor cars and even aeroplanes. Like Harold James, Thomas Humber had ceased association with his company by the time the motorised transport came into being, but he at least lived to see the motor vehicles bearing his name in popular use. Based at Beeston, Coventry and Wolverhampton in the Midlands of

England, the Humber works by the 1890s were responsible for most reputable bicycles and tricycles. 1892 was a significant year in the life of Humber. It was that year that Humber introduced the supported diamond frame which was adopted as standard by the cycle and motor cycle industry for the next sixty years. The company made its last ordinary or penny-farthing bicycle that year, and also made the most important change of all, when Thomas Humber resigned.

It was not until 1895 that the first experiments with engines were carried out at the Humber factory under the guiding influence of H. J. Lawson. Experiments were at this time also carried out for a short period on an electric tandem cycle. The first Humber experimental motor cycle was ready by 1896 based on the Kane-Pennington design, the patent of which Lawson purchased for £100,000. The experiment was a disaster. Success was to follow, however, with the manufacture of the popular Leon Bollee and De Dion type tricycles for which Lawson again held the patent rights.

1899 saw the introduction of the first four-wheel Humber, a De Dion type quadricycle followed by the M.D. quad with a single-cylinder engine driving the front wheels, while steering was supposedly achieved with the rear wheels.

The company re-formed in 1900 under different management as Humber Ltd., and the manufacture of motor cycles from that time was solely at the Coventry- or Beeston-based works. Humbers were experimenting with motor cars at the same time as motor cycles. The first Humber motor car proper entered the scene in 1901 and production of motor cycles began in 1902 with two models, one of which was belt-driven with a Minerva engine, and the other chain-driven. The latter was made under licence from Phelon and Moore and proved without doubt to be the finest design of its era. One of the most successful Humber motor tricycles was the Olympia Tandem which carried a passenger in a basket chair in front of the rider.

One aspect of the early Humber motor cycle which attracted attention was the use of the free engine clutch. By 1905 Humbers had entered the coach-built tricar scene with another Olympia model. Motor cycle production was suspended for four years between 1905 and 1909 due to the expansion of the motor car side of the business and a general recession in the motor cycle industry. They re-commenced with a $3\frac{1}{2}$ horsepower model followed closely by a 2 horsepower model. Although belt-driven, the $3\frac{1}{2}$ horsepower model had a two-speed Humber Roc epicyclic hub gear with starting handle and substantial band clutches. Its flexibility and reliability played a major part in the acceptance of the light sidecar as a means of sociable transport. That so many machines of the 1911–12 designs are still in existence is a clear testimony of their quality.

In motor cycle racing the greatest Humber success recorded must be P. J. Evans' victory in the 1911 Junior T.T. race in the Isle of Man, when he not only recorded the fastest lap average at 42 miles per hour but also finished over nine minutes ahead of his nearest rival, Harry Collier on the highly esteemed Matchless. Evan's Humber was a 342cc V-twin cylinder machine with belt drive and an Armstrong Triplex hub gear and was kept secret until the race when six such Humbers started and all finished. This model held the Brooklands record for 1911–12 for the 350cc class at 59 miles in the hour. Meanwhile the first regular air-mail service in the world was opened in India using Humber biplanes.

In 1913 an air-cooled motor cycle of 743cc was announced, with two small cylinders to the rear and one large one to the front giving perfect balance. Production difficulties permitted only six to be made, but the design was the forerunner of the 750cc water-cooled flat twin of 1915. This was dropped in 1916 in favour of a $3\frac{1}{2}$ horsepower air-cooled flat-twin as the sole Humber model. Car production ceased to allow the factory to concentrate on the manufacture of the Avro 504K and the BR2 nine-cylinder rotary aeroplane engine. Field kitchens and shells were additional war-time products of the Humber factory.

Motor cycle production re-commenced after the war with a $4\frac{1}{2}$ horse-power air-cooled flat twin which was continued until 1924 and in 1922 the first of a series of conventional $2\frac{3}{4}$ horsepower side-valve machines was introduced and this model continued in production until 1930. An over-head valve model was brought out in 1926 followed by an overhead camshaft 350cc model in 1928.

The latter part of the twenties proved a difficult time for most industries in Britain and financial problems brought several companies to their knees. In 1928 the Hillman factory, close neighbours of Humber, were bought out and it was not long before the directors at Humbers decided to discontinue motor cycles and concentrate on car production. In 1932 Rootes Ltd. took over, and the bicycle interest was sold to Raleigh, the famous Nottingham cycle manufacturers. The wheel had turned full circle.

23 HUSQVARNA

Like many other motorcycle manufacturers, Husqvarna developed from the bicycle trade, the transition occurring in 1903. Indeed the early models were very much like bicycles with the added encumbrance of an engine. The pedals, handlebars, frame, saddle and wheels of the first Husqvarna all had the distinctive appearance of the normal pedal cycle, and since the engine was imported from Belgium, in the beginning Husqvarna could not claim to be pathfinders in the motor cycling world. The first model was powered by the Belgian single-cylinder four-stroke $1\frac{1}{4}$ horsepower F.N. engine with belt drive to the rear wheel. It was claimed that speeds up to 50 kilometres per hour (25 to 30 miles per hour) could be achieved, although (as the instruction manual did warn the rider) there might be certain difficulties in starting the machine from cold. In that event the rider was urged to heat the carburettor 'by holding a burning newspaper under it' and the present day reader may wonder in what proportion machines and riders were lost in that way.

The Belgian engine was used until 1909 when investigation showed that perhaps another foreign manufacturer had a better product, namely Moto-Reve from Switzerland. In fact this change did not prove entirely successful as the Moto-Reve engines were not quite as reliable as the tried and proven F.N. engines. However for about ten years Husqvarna continued an occasionally strained relationship with Moto-Reve. During this period, apart from introducing the twin-cylinder engine, progress at Husqvarna was marked by the introduction of all-chain-drive from as early as 1909 and kick-start mechanism.

Husqvarna's driving force for so long was Gustaf Tham, their managing director from 1911 until 1946, who not only encouraged the development of the machine but also urged the company into motor cycling competition on the basis that success would be the best advertisement to sell the product. At first success was only achieved on a national basis, but this was better than nothing. As early as 1916 Husqvarna were able to produce a sufficiently reliable and tough motor cycle to win the Swedish Novemberkasan (November Trophy) Trial and indeed take second and third places as well. With their growing reputation came an order to supply the Swedish Army with motor cycles, which proved to be a much-needed financial fillip.

It was not until about 1919/1920 that Husqvarna put on the market a motor cycle completely manufactured by themselves. While there had been satisfactory results from the early machines with the Belgian and Swiss engines, Husqvarna naturally wanted to be entirely independent and to put out a motor cycle which could be called Husqvarna through and through. Their first engine was a side valve four-stroke twin-cylinder, and the first model provided the rider with a most comfortable ride, the accent being placed upon springing which was so important in the days when roads were not as smooth as today's. Another innovation on the model was the optional alternative to the lever controlled throttle, the twist grip throttle. The 'complete' Husqvarna was however short-lived because it cost more to make the engines than import them. By the mid-twenties the company reverted to purchasing foreign-made engines and this time looked in the direction of England. Husqvarna considered their 'best buy' to be J.A.P. engines although they toyed with Sturmey Archer (Raleigh) for a short period.

From the beginning of this decade, sidecars had been available as the motor cycle was used not only by the sporting man but also by the family man in Sweden. There were the wickerwork basket-type sidecars and also the most modern aluminium bullet-shaped style to give the rider some choice in the matter.

1936 was a significant year in the life of Husqvarna. The 500cc four-stroke single-cylinder o.h.v. model known as the 112TV was introduced to the public. It was regarded as the epitome of all that Husqvarna motor cycle manufacturing stood for, and it also heralded the end for a long period of time of their 'big bike' production. In 1938 the factory changed its policy to concentrate on production of the lightweight motor cycles which are so popular even today throughout the continent of Europe. In 1938, however, Calle Heimdahl, whose inspiration led to this dramatic change of policy, was setting the trend. His theory that the general public would quickly take to an easy-to-handle light and economical motor cycle proved absolutely correct. Perhaps he anticipated that with another world war such a machine would be worth its weight in gold. The model 301, with its 98cc engine and two-speed gearbox was quickly modified in the next two or three years to eliminate the bicycle pedals and to include foot-rests with a kick-starter. The 'Svartkvarnan' 118cc, a three-speed two-stroke single-cylinder motor cycle, followed in its footsteps and was sufficiently popular to warrant production until 1954. Husqvarna were the European fore-runners of Honda and remarkably successful in the small motor cycle field.

On the road race track prior to the Second World War, success had been limited to national level with a few wins in the Swedish Grand Prix in the nineteen thirties and little else, with the result that the works team was disbanded. However it was discovered, as with other makes renowned for reliability, that if racing on the road was not their particular forte, trials and moto-cross could be. The fact that Husqvarna concentrated on the light-weight motor cycle was not necessarily a handicap in these fields and considerable success was achieved at international level, including six first class awards in the 1953 International Six Days Trial on their 175cc machines.

The modified Silverpil (Silver Arrow) 250cc with three-speed gearbox was used with formidable success in moto-cross including making a win possible for Sweden in the 1959 European Championship. Originally the Silverpil was manufactured to meet the market of the sixteen-year-olds in Sweden who were limited by law to riding motor cycles of 75 kilograms or less and the 175cc Silverpil was specially designed for them. Indeed the 'road racing appearance' of the bike was guaranteed to attract the young enthusiast. With these achievements behind them the management at Husqvarna were encouraged to dabble once more with the larger machinery for competition purposes and 'dusted down' their pride and joy of the thirties, the 112TV. This remarkable machine, once modified, immediately helped Bill Nilsson ride off with the 1960 500cc World Moto-Cross Championship and Totte Halman won four individual 500cc Moto-Cross Championships. This if nothing else shows the tough quality, reliability and speed of the machines – 'Husky' by name and it would seem by nature also.

24 INDIAN

At the turn of the century George M. Hendee was a successful manufacturer of pedal cycles and an enthusiast of pedal cycle races. He was the founder of the Hendee Manufacturing Company in Springfield, Massachusetts, in the USA and owned a half-interest in a cycle race track. It was this combination which attracted George Hendee to the idea of making motor cycles. The racing cyclists at this time were in many events paced by motorised tandem cycles of an extremely unreliable nature, with the result that many races were spoiled by the pacing machines which failed at vital moments and left the racers stranded. In 1900, he succeeded in finding a more reliable machine to do this work, made and ridden by one Oscar Hedstrom and it occurred to Hendee that by combining forces they might go successfully into business as motor cycle manufacturers. The contractual formalities were confined simply to one hand-written note and the Indian motor-cycle was conceived in the first month of 1901. George Hendee arranged finances and organised the experimental workshops out in Connecticut, laying down certain principles to which the motor cycles must adhere. Both Hendee and Hedstrom were adamant that any machine built by them must have quality as the foremost consideration, although the purpose of the machine was to provide a motor cycle for the masses. Hedstrom was to be in charge of design and construction and the first Indian motor cycle was on the road later in the year of 1901. From the outset, the machine was christened Indian by Hendee and he insisted that it should be painted red. The spell was cast and the 'magic of the red steed of steel' was about to spread. The prototype Indian was a small $1\frac{3}{4}$ horsepower single-cylinder machine with a basic appearance of a pedal cycle, incorporating pedals and chain-drive. The light high-compression engine formed part of the frame below the saddle and features of the machine were Hedstrom's own special spray-type concentric float carburettor and the battery ignition. From the first the machine was noted for its smooth and quiet performance.

With an eye to future export sales Hendee sent one of the very first Indians to a large motor cycle show in Great Britain in 1901 and set about developing production possibilities. Hendee knew from experience that there is no better advertisement than proving the goods you sell in public and in the first American road race in 1902 at Brooklyn, New York, an Indian was ridden to victory by George Holden in what must have been a record time. While in trials and hill climbs Indians took many 'scalps' including a remarkable first, second and third place in the coveted but gruelling New York to Boston trial covering about 280 miles of difficult terrain, the riders being Hendee, Hedstrom and Holden. By the end of the year demand for Indians far exceeded their output of about 140, but Hendee and Hedstrom were not tempted into making the 'quick buck' by taking short cuts at manufacturing level. The Indian standard motor cycle remained basically the same in design until 1905 when the single-cylinder machine was modified to take twist grip control for carburettor and ignition and spring or cushion forks were introduced. The twist grip system was operated from both hand-grips, the right operating the spark and exhaust valve, while the left operated the throttle. Another model joined the team, a twin-cylinder 490cc machine, making it the first twin-cylinder motor cycle in production in the USA, although it was not marketed for another two years. It was particularly successful in sporting competitions. With greater production came the need for larger premises for the factory and in the same year the Indian motor cycle production commenced in a large old school building in Springfield which was converted into a factory. That school building remained the basis of all future Indian factory expansion although by the time of the last addition in 1931 it would have been difficult to find the original building in the vast estate.

For 1906 the single-cylinder became a $2\frac{1}{4}$ horsepower machine and by 1908 the single-cylinder was alternatively $2\frac{3}{4}$, $3\frac{1}{2}$ or 4 horsepower while 5 or 7 horsepower twin-cylinder models were also obtainable. Other options open to the purchaser were belt- or chain-drive, battery or magneto ignition and automatic or mechanical inlet valves. The little $2\frac{3}{4}$ horsepower model capable of speeds up to about 45 miles per hour was sold at a basic price of two hundred dollars, with the optional extras improving both performance and price. The most expensive model was the 7 horsepower twin-cylinder machine with its racing position for riders including toe clips on the pedals, capable of speeds up to sixty-five miles per hour. This cost the purchaser a basic three hundred and fifty dollars.

The famous 'red steeds' could in fact be purchased in alternative colours of royal blue or black. The married man or modern Casanova could purchase an Indian Tricar to enable him to take a passenger in comfort. Indians allowed for the addition of a pillion seat behind the rider on standard models, but for the more sedate journey the tricar provided the answer. A single tricar could be purchased for about three hundred and twenty-five dollars while the twin-cylinder model cost an extra fifty. The upholstered passenger chair rode between the two front wheels while the rider sat behind over the solitary rear wheel. Difficulties in manufacture had been experienced at the outset of production of the tricar in 1905 but with the invention of the Indian independent helical spring suspension the solution was found to provide adequate comfort for the passenger and stability to the machine.

For 1909 the major change was the substitution of a loop cradle frame for the twin-cylinder models.

With an eye to overseas markets Hedstrom pushed Indians into European competitions and in 1911 hit the jackpot, when Indian became the first make to capture the top three places in the Isle of Man T.T. races. The Indians were also the first winners of the Senior T.T. since it was only introduced that year. The team of O. C. Godfrey, C. B. Franklin and A. Moorhouse pulverised the opposition with the exception of Charles Collier on his Matchless who was disqualified from second place on a breach of race regulations. The result had the desired result of boosting world sales. The following year an eighth place was the best they could muster. Honour was once more salvaged by A. H. Alexander with a third place in 1913 and O. C. Godfrey's second place (a joint place with the young Howard Davies) in the 1914 event. The major addition to the Indian range of that year was the Hendee Special with its revolutionary electrically operated starter and lighting equipment.

Mention should be made at this stage of the remarkable achievements of two famous Indian riders, C. B. Franklin and 'Cannonball' Baker. Franklin had demonstrated the formidable speed of the Indian two years earlier when he made a record-breaking run of 300 miles in as many minutes over the celebrated Brooklands track in England. Baker demonstrated the endurance and reliability of the Indians on many runs including one which set the Coast-to-Coast record in 1914. This trip of 3,300 miles of unpaved road was a severe test for both man and machine and Baker and his Indian Twin made it in 11 days 11 hours.

A new designer came to the forefront of Indian production in 1914, Charles Gustafson, a former speedway rider. He was responsible for the 'Power-plus' motor which quickly overcame initial sceptism and went into general production in 1916. By that time it had already taken many world records for distance covered in specific times and won many national hill climbs, trials and road races. Again Baker was to prove the worth of the Power-plus in 1917 with his wonderful 'Twenty-four Hours' record run of 1,534 miles, which he held for several years until Wells Bennett came along on a Henderson X in 1922. The Hendee Manufacturing Company were by now concentrating attention on twin-cylinder motor cycles rather than the single-cylinder machines. It was during 1916 that George M. Hendee retired from the company.

The 1917 range prior to the United States entry into the First World War included a 7 horsepower model and a lighter $2\frac{1}{2}$ horsepower model, both with three-speed gearboxes and still featuring the cradle spring frame together with triple-stem front forks. The machine was wanted immediately for the American war effort and over forty thousand olive-drab coloured Indians were used by the American forces during the remainder of the war.

A shot in the arm for post-war Indian production was the arrival of C. B. Franklin hot from the racing stable to assist at the drawing board. His 500cc 'Scout' V-twin-cylinder side valve machine was soon to become, according to Indian advertisements, the 'world's most popular twin solo motor cycle'. Later in the year a bigger 1000cc Powerplus version with rear suspension was added to the range. In road racing circles, Freddie Dixon and Herbert le Vack took second and third places for Indian in the second post-war Senior T.T. The first place was taken by a 350cc A.J.S. ridden by Howard Davies. Two years later in 1923 Freddie Dixon had to be content with third place before he changed his racing stable for succeeding events, and Indian ceased to race in the Isle of Man. The major innovation of the early twenties was the 'Big' Chief, superseding the 1000cc Power plus, a 1200cc V-twin-cylinder side valve monster. In the early twenties balloon tyres were most popular throughout the United States and were naturally featured on Indian models. By the mid-twenties Indian could claim the motor cycle speed record with Paul Anderson's 125 miles per hour down in Australia and this was increased to 132 miles per hour in 1926 at Daytona Beach, Florida, in the USA with John Seymour in the saddle. In the same year Indian brought out another single-cylinder model with three-speed, called the Indian Prince, featuring a new keystone frame in two sections and this model proved itself all over the world in major trials events.

1927 saw the company take over W. G. Henderson's Ace Motor Cycles and put the Indian Ace into production. In the 1928–9 season Indian motor cycles cleared the board in all United States National championship racing events.

The Indian Ace reappeared in the guise of the Indian Four in 1929 and remained in production until the Second World War. The prominent features of the Indian at the start of the 1930s were the touring handlebars with crossbar and heavy spoked wheels on all models. The modifications and improvements made during the next decade did not greatly affect the design or performance of the machines and no new model was offered. The thirties were a hard time economically for people in the USA whether they were manufacturers or prospective purchasers, and to make expensive new models would be money wasted in the design department followed by difficulties in selling the finished product. Once again, Indians produced motor cycles for the troops, in the Second World War, and celebrated the cease-fire with a new single-cylinder model, the 230cc overhead valve 'Arrow'. The 1000cc 'Big Chief' model continued with the ever popular 'Scout'. For 1950 a variation on the Scout model was brought into production for a short time, the Warrior, a 500cc vertical overhead twin-cylinder machine.

However, in the early fifties the Indian Motor Cycle Company was no longer a financially viable proposition and an English-based company, Brockhouse Engineering Company, took over production in 1953. For six years a motor cycle under the name of Indian was manufactured in the north of England, and then this last interest in the Indian motor cycle concern was swallowed up by Associated Motor Cycles Ltd., of London, England, who were basically the Matchless Motor Cycle Company. It was ironical that Indian advertising of 1917 should have referred to its very own Powerplus and light twin-cylinder machines as 'the Team of Matchless Motor Cycles'. Ridden by enthusiasts throughout the world for over fifty years, successfully raced in all the major championships, used extensively by the American armed forces, state police forces and motor cycle fire patrols, used by countless commercial concerns throughout the world for delivery purposes either as solos or with sidecars, Indian motor cycles were a major force in their time and will never be forgotten.

25 JAMES

In one respect at least James must be considered almost unique. The man whose name adorns the motor cycle, Harold James, was not responsible for any motor cycle at all. He had in fact died prior to the manufacture of the first. Harold James was a man whose interest in bicycles began with the 'penny farthing' and the business of their manufacture from about 1880. He was a small one-man, one-room, business in the beginning but developed over the following decade into a prosperous organisation. He was yet one more Midlander involved in the two-wheel transport business, his work-shops being situated in Birmingham. In 1897 the James Cycle Co., was sufficiently large and successful to be turned from a private into a public company, and with the transformation Harold James quietly retired from the scene. When the first James motor cycle was produced in 1902, Harold James had passed away. The man largely responsible for this James motor cycle was Frederick Kimberley, who, prior to his engagement by the James Cycle Company, had experience with other pioneer motor cycle organisations and was able to take the benefit of that knowledge with him. In the first year of production there were two models of James motor cycles. Like many of their contemporaries, the basis of the machine was a bicycle with an engine added to provide the power. However while the model 'A' had belt drive, the Model 'B' had a slightly less usual device for driving the rear wheel. This consisted of a small short chain from engine to a friction roller which was held in contact with the rear tyre. The model 'B' was powered by a Derby motor and the model 'A' was driven by the popular Minerva. Either model could be purchased for £55.

The following year only one model James was available for purchase the model 'T'. This was a $2\frac{1}{2}$ horsepower Minerva machine, with belt drive retailing for a slightly lower price of £50. If these prices sound cheap by today's standards, it should be remembered that at the beginning of the century a sum like this would constitute the average working man's yearly income.

In 1904 James first introduced the loop frame to hold the Belgian-made F.N. engine. It was not original, of course, having been previously used. In 1908 however James contributed original ideas in motor cycle construction with the 'Safety' model, the brainchild of P. L. Renouf. This machine had an open frame with running boards instead of foot-rests or pedals. The wheels were fitted on spindles so that they could be changed easily in days when punctures were the everyday occurrence on poor quality roads. Brake shoes in the hubs expanded to retard the vehicle's progress. The saddle was long and made more comfortable by leaf springs, and the machine was powered by the first James engine, a four-stroke, which had inlet and exhaust valves worked one within the other. The 'Safety' model was to stay for several years and caused changes in the models produced by many of their rivals. In 1911 James reverted to a traditional frame but sported a two-speed countershaft gearbox, a multi-plate clutch, chain-drive, kick-start and shock absorbers.

In 1911 James made their first takeover, swallowing up the Osmond company who made lightweight motor cycles.

Prior to the First World War, James were successfully producing a lightweight two-stroke solo machine, a $4\frac{1}{2}$ horsepower single-cylinder model so popular among sidecar owners especially when used with their own home-made 'Canoelet' model and a twin-cylinder model for the speedy rider, called the 'Famous James', a $3\frac{1}{2}$ horsepower 500cc machine. James contributed to the war effort with motor cycles used by the Belgian and Russian forces.

Post-war production was interrupted by a fire at the factory which put the company out of action for a couple of years. They resumed with 250cc and 350cc models, both side valve machines in the James tradition, and 500cc side and overhead valve V-twin models later in the twenties. The second takeover made by James came in 1930 when the Baker firm responsible for lightweight motor cycles were hit by the financial difficulties overwhelming so many companies in the motor cycling industry. James lightweight motor cycles were now being powered by Villiers engines, and from about 1930 onwards the company concentrated on the production of two-stroke models in the range 98cc to 250cc.

During the Second World War the factory made munitions and aircraft components and also turned out two-stroke autocycles specially adapted for invasion forces. Post-war production carried on mainly with lightweight models but the company that had taken over other less fortunate motor cycle firms in the past was now overtaken by its own financial misfortunes. In the early fifties it was merged with Associated Motor Cycles Ltd., the Matchless-controlled organisation. From that date machines marketed under the name of James were lightweight models up to 250cc and motor scooters. If Harold James had known about the motor cycles produced under his name, he would have had no cause to be dissatisfied with the contribution they have made to the history of the British motor cycle.

26 KAWASAKI

The first Kawasaki motor cycle was produced in Japan in 1968, making it the most 'junior' make in this book. However the company itself has a considerable history in many other fields of engineering. The Kawasaki company was founded in a dockyard in Tokyo in 1878. The man responsible for the company was Shozo Kawasaki, but the thought of manufacturing motor cycles was not in his mind at this time. Soon after the turn of the century the Kawasaki Dockyard began to diversify its manufacturing interests by building locomotives, freight cars, coaches and bridge trusses, and entered into the marine transportation business. Over the years the company interests continued to expand so that at the present time the company has interests in production of ships and aircraft, rolling stock and commercial vehicles as well as many other products requiring engineering skill and expertise.

The motor cycle division of Kawasaki was started in 1968 at the time of the general regrouping of Kawasaki companies and the founding of Kawasaki Heavy Industries Ltd. At the present time Kawasaki motor cycles are exported to as many as ninety different countries throughout the world, and with the increasing demand has come the realisation that assembly plants in countries other than Japan are necessary to satisfy that demand. The company plan such expansion in many countries including Nigeria, the Philippines and the USA and with the opening of such a plant in America it will be another 'first' for Kawasaki as no other Japanese motor cycle manufacturer will have done this. The main Kawasaki works are at Akashi situated about four hundred miles south-west of Tokyo and alongside the Inland Sea. This plant was established in 1930 originally for the manufacture of aeroplane engines and fuselage components. Now the motor cycle production line there claims to produce a motor cycle every fifty seconds and their popularity world wide is such that over 96 per cent of motor cycles produced are sold abroad.

The Kawasaki range of motor cycles includes machines of 125, 250, 400, 500, 750 and 900cc. All have five-speed gearboxes with the exception of the 125cc. All machines are two-stroke, for which the Japanese are justly famous, with the exception of the 900cc which is a double overhead camshaft four-stroke.

On the racing scene Kawasaki quickly made the victory rostrum in the Isle of Man T.T. races, with first place going to Dave Simmons on his 125cc machine in the Ultra Lightweight race of 1969. The overwhelming success the company gained on the United States of America road racing tracks in 1973 must have been particularly satisfying for a factory with relatively little experience. The future looks interesting for Kawasaki.

27 LEA-FRANCIS

By the end of the nineteenth century R. H. Lea and his business partner, G. I. Francis, were responsible for one of the most famous pedal cycles in Great Britain. Like so many engineers, their factory was based in Coventry, in the Midlands region of England. The Lea-Francis safety bicycle provided them with a prosperous income and a showroom in the smartest part of Piccadilly in London. The advent of the internal combustion engine interested and intrigued them. Like Thomas Humber and John Marston of Sunbeam, they took the difficult but fascinating step from pedal to motor bicycles. However, Lea and Francis made the transition through experiment with motor cars and subsequent car manufacture from about 1903. This postponed the taking of the step until it was actually negotiated in 1911. The prototype Lea-Francis, designed by Ingle with assistance from the young Norman Lea, was not ready until the following year. The first Lea-Francis motor cycle was a 430cc J.A.P.-engined side valve, twin-cylinder machine, with two-speed gearbox and dummy rim front brake.

The company was determined to maintain the high standard of quality expected of Lea-Francis machines.

By 1914 the motor cycle side of the business was in full production of 430cc, 500cc and 750cc twin-cylinder machines. The engines used were either the home-produced J.A.P. or the Swiss M.A.G., but after the First World War it seems that J.A.P. engines were never used again for the Lea-Francis. The pre-war Lea-Francis 430cc twin-cylinder machine could be purchased for the sum of £69 10s (£69.50) and was generally regarded as value for money.From the beginning Lea-Francis favoured foot-boards rather than foot-rests. For the protection of the rider from mud and water thrown up off the roads, enclosed mudguards with mudshield at the front were fitted together with an under-tray which swung forward to double as a front stand. There was a completely encased chain and easily detachable front and rear wheels enabled rapid repairs. The R.H. Lea patent reflex lamp at the rear provided better illumination.

The First World War brought production to a standstill and with the end of hostilities Lea-Francis resumed where they had left off. G. I. Francis took a close interest in his son's motor cycle company Francis and·Barnett Ltd., becoming a director of that company as well. Gordon Francis, the son of G. I. (Graham) Francis was busy at that time with Arthur Barnett in emulating his father's success and the family Francis have certainly earned a niche for themselves in the history of British motor cycles.

The post-war Lea-Francis continued the format as before, with only slight modifications such as the optional improvements to the braking system. The firm, with its spreading reputation, believed that the satisfied customer would repeat his order in due time and would know all about the product he was buying. Its handling in adverse weather and road conditions was proved by the success of the Lea-Francis in trials events. Graham Francis, young Norman Lea with A. J. Sproston all had notable successes on the Lea-Francis in many major events including the Scottish Six Days Trials. Perhaps the great reliability of Lea-Francis precipitated the end of motor cycle production, since satisfied customers had no need to renew their machines.

In 1920 a 592cc model with three-speed gearbox was put on the market for sidecar purposes, and a sporting model costing in the region of £110 was developed for 1922. By 1924 it was decided to close down the motor cycle side of the business and concentrate on the light motor car trade where business was starting to boom. In all forms of wheeled transport, Lea and Francis produced quality, class and style and the owners of their pedal cycles, motor cycles and motor cars always appreciated the fact. Compared with other motor cycle companies the Lea-Francis output may have been small, but quality counts for more than quantity.

28 LEVIS

In the annals of British motor cycle history the name Levis is synonymous with two-stroke lightweight machines. The Butterfield brothers aided and abetted by Howard Newey, were pioneers of two-stroke motor cycles and set a standard for others to aim at. Others did eventually pass that standard but this cannot obscure the early achievement of the Butterfield/Newey organisation. Stephenson's steam engine and Ford's idea of the popular motor car were superseded but this does not detract from the importance of their original work.

William and Arthur Hughes Butterfield opened up business in 1906 as engineers, initially with no motor cycle connections other than a natural interest in developments in engineering progress. William started experimenting with engines of his own design and by 1910 had a successful two-stroke engine on the stocks. By 1911 he and his brother were established as motor cycle manufacturers. The name chosen for the motor cycles produced by them came from a classical education – Levis meaning 'light' as in lightweight. The firm's motto from the start was 'levis et celer', and in their day the Levis motor cycle certainly proved to be both light and speedy.

The first Levis set the standard which the Butterfields aimed at maintaining throughout their firm's life. It was a 198cc single-cylinder two-stroke machine with belt-drive and pedalling apparatus, fitted on a bicycle-type frame with bicycle saddle and handlebars. It weighed a mere 85 pounds and was capable of speeds up to about 35 miles per hour.

From the earliest days the Butterfield brothers were given the most able support by Howard (Bob) Newey who is considered by some to be worthy of the title 'Mr Levis', since he contributed so much to the design and development of the Levis motor cycle over the next thirty years or so. He also tuned the racing machines for the works team and in the early days even raced them himself. If William Butterfield was king at Levis, Newey was certainly the Prime Minister. The prototype Levis was modified for sale and the Model Number 1 was a slightly larger 269cc version and the second model to follow in production was the 211cc Baby Levis. The purchase price of each was about £35 10s (£35.50) and £33 10s (£33.50) respectively. Fourteen or fifteen years later, the purchase price of a Levis two-stroke was less than £30. What product of the 1970s will cost less to buy in the 1980s?

1913 was the year of incorporation at Levis, the little firm becoming Butterfields Ltd. The brothers were directors of the company and Howard Newey took the reins as works manager. The models for that year were merely variations on the now popular theme, with relatively minor alterations. These included a lowered riding position and a version of the Model 1 with alternative chain/belt-drive while the Baby Levis and standard Model 1 continued faithfully with belt-drive. The idea of mounting two of their two-stroke engines side by side on one machine with a single common crankcase never really caught on and was quickly dropped.

The business prospered and the company decided to extend their range of machines. For the following year a 349cc De Luxe model was conceived at the De Luxe retail price of £42. For the man with a little less cash to spare, the Popular model, a 211cc, was introduced, while the Baby Levis and the Model 1 with variations continued in harness.

The First World War naturally slowed both production and demand, but the early post-war era showed a healthy demand for lightweight motor cycles. This demand was repeated after the cease-fire of the Second World War, but on that occasion Levis decided not to fulfil it. Rekindling the fires in 1919, the Butterfields made several innovations to attract the customers. Over the early post-war years Levis introduced better gear-boxes mainly of Burman manufacture, internal expanding brakes, kick-starters and mechanical oil pumps. There were now many keen rivals in the two-stroke market as the day of the two-stroke was seen to have arrived, but Levis had experience which counted for much in the early twenties. At that time the competitors were still discovering the difficulties already overcome at Butterfields some eight or nine years before.

If their motto was 'light and quick' they soon changed their sales pro-duction slogan to 'The Master Two-Stroke' and endeavoured to prove this both in production of standard models and also in road racing. Prior to the war the Butterfield concern had dabbled in road racing but the lack of races for machines of 200cc or 250cc was hardly encouraging. There were a few road races in Europe but little on the domestic front, and they had really only been able to show their prowess in Britain in trials, where they had quickly gained a great reputation. Having demonstrated their reliability and endurance, the challenge to prove their speed – and the firm's motto – was irresistible. Fortunately the growing interest in lightweight motor cycles in the early post-war days gave the necessary impetus to the authorities to include a 250cc class in the Junior event of the 1920 Isle of Man T.T. races. Levis were anxious to live up to their new claim of 'The Master Two-Stroke'.

The 250cc trophy was offered for the best performance by a machine of 250cc or less in the Junior T.T., which of course consisted for the most part of 350cc machines. It says something for the Levis 250 that for most of the race R. O. Clark was in contention for first place amongst the 350 machines. In the end he finished in fourth place overall and was the clear winner of the 250cc class, despite the minor handicap of a crash during the last lap. This left his front wheel so buckled that he had to do on-the-spot repairs to make the wheel revolve again on the spindle, allowing him to coast gently round the remainder of the course in order to reach the finishing line. To prove the point Levis took second and third places in the 250cc class with the remarkable veteran rider F. W. (Pa) Applebee in the saddle of the latter. At the age of fifty-eight, it was a formidable task to ride around the $187\frac{1}{2}$-mile course let alone be placed the third rider in his class. He held the record for the oldest competitor in these events when he finally competed in the 1922 Lightweight race, but only for two years until G. Cowley took the 'title' at the age of sixty-one in the Junior race of 1924.

Geoff Davison is an important name in Levis racing history. He took consecutive Grand Prix titles on his Levis in Belgium and France in 1922 and 1923, and won a gold medal in the International Six Days trial on the smallest machine in the field. He also led the first Lightweight race in the Isle of Man T.T. in 1922, coming in thirteen minutes ahead of his nearest rival, after he had narrowly failed to win the year before in the Junior 250cc event. On that occasion a broken belt deprived him of the winning position and left him in a dignified second place. Davison and Levis went hand-in-hand, and loyalty to the company may well have deprived the rider of greater success later in the twenties. As the decade wore on, the rival two-stroke manufacturers rapidly made up lost ground and even if the standard Levis machine was probably more reliable and better value for the customer than the majority of the faster makes, by 1923 it was no longer the swiftest. Levis performances in races rapidly declined. The 1923 model was not up to scratch and in competitions the riders continued on the old 1922 machines. Levis hopes rose when an Ultra-Lightweight class in the Isle of Man T.T. races was introduced in 1924 for machines of under 175cc. The Levis 'Copper-Nob' was developed with great enthusiasm and the fourth place it successfully gained in the race was regarded at Levis as a total failure. The company never seriously competed in the major road races again (with one disastrous exception later in the decade), and concentrated on producing new models to attract the customers in the shops.

The 1924 'K' was an expensive little 250cc model with chain-drive, three-speed gearbox and a top speed of 50 miles per hour. It was a step taken towards chain-driven machines while Levis was still generally adhering to a belt-drive policy. The model M of the following year catered for the man with less money to spend and was just a cheaper version of the model K. Over the next couple of years Levis was able to make sufficient money-saving amendments to bring the purchase price of the machine down even further. By 1927 the model M was re-named the Levisette (not to be confused with the similarly named 1914 model of 175cc) and cost under £29. Both the model K and the Levisette went out of production before the end of the decade, suffering badly in comparison with the earlier Popular which, living up to its name, continued to be manufactured for over eleven years. It only went out of the catalogue when a 'new broom' attitude at management level demanded new models in 1924.

Other new Levis models of the mid-twenties were the Model 'O', a 247cc two-stroke for sporting purposes, and the Model 'A', introduced in 1926 with a distinctive flat tank and three-speed Burman gearbox. The latter was modified before the end of the decade to take a saddle tank, and then a four-speed gearbox and two upswept exhaust pipes to keep in with the common trend. The first 'six port' 250cc two-stroke model was brought out in 1928, yet another to be taken out of production by 1930. During the thirties the accent at Levis was uncharacteristically on four-stroke models. They even made a 500cc and 600cc machine, both overhead valve single-cylinder machines. The Levis policy was never to confuse economy with cheap quality and high standards were always set to the very end. During the thirties a 250cc overhead camshaft model was produced, a swan song for the company. With the arrival of the Second World War, the factory was taken over for the manufacture of aircraft parts. This too was in keeping with Levis tradition as the design and manufacture o aeroplane engines were among the experiments in the pre-First World War era at Butterfield's Birmingham workshops. These happy days of motor cycle pioneering must have seemed a far cry from the life and death battle being waged above them in 1940. For Levis motor cycles, as for so much else, the war heralded the end.

29 MARTINSYDE

Unlike so many other motor cycle collaborators, Helmuth Paul Martin and George Harris Handasyde were not drawn together by their mutual interest in machines on two wheels. Their first love was flying and they joined forces in the first decade of the century solely to make aircraft. Their early ventures were very advanced and successful, for they seriously considered the possibility of a Martinsyde monoplane crossing the Atlantic before the First World War intervened to change their priorities. Naturally the Government looked to Martin and Handasyde for air assistance and found it in their fighter planes. The firm grew in staff and took over new premises for carrying out orders. However, with the cease-fire the demand for aircraft died and Martin and Handasyde looked round for new ways of using their equipment and staff. With the assistance of the motor cycle engine specialist Howard C. Newman (of Ivy fame), Martinsyde metaphorically changed horses (or at least horsepower).

The prototype Martinsyde–Newman was ready by 1919 and the first models left the factory in 1920. In the same year Newman also left the factory and the motor cycles produced thereafter were just called Martinsyde. The 1920 machines were 678cc and 500cc models both being two-cylinder V-twin-engined machines with A.J.S.-type gearboxes, and Brampton forks. By 1922 a sports model called the 'Quick Six' was also being produced with a slightly more powerful engine and a distinctive round tank. However, the firm was already beset with problems that eventually proved to be its downfall. Perhaps because of their relative inexperience, machine production was slower than demand with the result that customers grew impatient with waiting. A strike by their suppliers added greatly to the delay. The result was that a large number of customers cancelled their orders, causing the firm heavy financial losses Business picked up to a certain extent in 1921, mainly because those machines which did eventually get off the production line and into the customers' hands proved to be of such good quality that customers were appeased and their reputation grew.

Conveniently situated in their factory near Brooklands, it is not surprising that even in their few years of manufacture Martinsyde machines should have achieved a certain amount of success on the famous circuit, notably in the 500-mile race and in breaking the speed record over one hour. The greatest achievement credited to the machines must be the five gold medals in the 1922 Six Days Trial. Their newly found success was short-lived and the death blow came when a fire started in the workshops and destroyed equipment. The fire in fact did not cause much damage and indeed if it had been more extensive substantial insurance compensation might have helped to turn the tide in the firm's favour.

The 350cc model had no opportunity to prove its worth or save the firm's fortunes, as only six machines ever left the premises. Bankrupt, the company finally ceased production in 1923. Such engines as were usable at the factory were purchased by Bat motor cycles for use in their own machines. For Martinsyde it was a short but worthwhile reign.

30 MATCHLESS

For Matchless, like many other firms, the entry into motor cycle manufacture was a natural progress from the production of bicycles late in the nineteenth century. The Collier brothers, H. A. (Harry) and C. R. (Charlie), made their first motor-powered bicycle in 1899. Indeed in those early years the machines were very much bicycles with the addition of engines placed wherever the maker could find room. The early Matchless motor cycles produced at the turn of the century had the engine placed between the saddle tube and the rear wheel, but by 1903 the engine had been moved forward, in front of and under the front down tube of the frame and behind the front wheel. Pedals were still provided, of course, to assist the engine on steep inclines or when it failed to function. The early Matchless motor cycles were driven by de Dion Bouton, J.A.P. and even M.M.C. engines. The production took place in their small factory in Plumstead, South-East London, and was forward-looking from the start. Pioneers are experimenters by nature, and with the motor cycle still in its infancy, the Collier brothers started to make a tri-car. The principle was that two front wheels replaced the normal single wheel, in order to support the wicker-work or metal carriage for the passenger, while the driver sat on the normal saddle and looked past his passenger at the highway ahead. So he became the original back seat driver.

The 1904 Matchless tri-car was in fact only a follow-up to other machines of quite similar appearance to those which had been manufactured since the beginning of the century under a variety of names. Where the Colliers showed great originality was in their early attempts at rear springing on motor cycles. The 1906 V-twin was equipped with a swinging fork sprung rear frame, the spring unit being placed under the saddle with links to the main frame.

Pioneers in every way, the Colliers entered the first Isle of Man T.T. races in 1907 and won the single-cylinder class with Charlie Collier naturally riding his own marque. In the same race Harry Collier put in the fastest recorded lap by a single-cylinder machine at 41·18 m.p.h. and Charlie's average speed over the $158\frac{1}{2}$-mile course was 38·22. In the 1908 T.T. event Charlie Collier had to be content with second place, but in that year a Matchless V-twin recorded a shattering 70 m.p.h. at the Brooklands track. In 1909 Harry Collier took over the winning formula from his brother and won the only T.T. event, the two classes having been merged into one. If the motor cycling world thought the Colliers had made their point, in 1910 they emphasised it again in a devastating first and second place, once more in the only T.T. race of the year. While speeds averaged about 50 m.p.h. per lap one must remember that greater skill was needed in those days to keep the machine running (and running smoothly) over 158 miles of poorly surfaced roads. Good fortune did not favour them the following year, and Harry Collier could do no better on his J.A.P.-engined single-cylinder machine than second place in the Junior event. Meanwhile Charlie Collier was disqualified in the Senior for filling his machine with petrol on the road when he ran out, and but for this would have taken another second place. At subsequent top-level road racing events Matchless were not successful although they achieved many trials and moto-cross victories to their credit.

Up to the First World War the Colliers were always anxious to be in at the start of any new motor cycling experiment, and along with many of their rivals they produced a cycle-car. This was a natural successor to the earlier tri-car but resembled the form of a motor car much more closely. The Matchless cycle-car was not so successful as the Morgan, which was generally recognised as reigning supreme in this field, nor as cheap since even then it cost over £100. The most distinctive feature of the Matchless cycle-car was its independent front wheel suspension with separate leaf springs, and a single transverse tube between the front wheels curving down in the centre to form a loop for the crank-case of the J.A.P. V-twin engine. The production of the Matchless cycle-car ceased in the mid-twenties with the arrival of the popualr mass-produced small motor car, which gave the family man greater space for his passengers and cost no more than the cycle-car. At the same time as the cycle-car was produced, Matchless sidecar outfits were popular with the public. Although sportsmen themselves, the Colliers did not forget that the motor cycle was a vehicle of transport as well as a competitive machine.

In the 1920s there were as many as eleven models to choose from in the Matchless range, powered from the small 246cc side valve up to the mighty 1000cc V-twin, all of which were now Matchless-made. Like many contemporaries at the end of that decade, the new Matchless machines appeared with white panels on their tanks.

The 1930 Silver Arrow was only in production for three years but during that time it made a remarkable impact. This model was manufactured with the man in the street in mind rather than the racing specialist or trials rider. It was designed strictly for transport purposes with a quiet side valve V-twin 400cc engine. The rider was given a speedy and comfortable journey on the machine's sprung rear frame. Its chromium and white tank was in keeping with the current trend. It was for obvious reasons nicknamed the 'Whispering Wonder'. The Silver Arrow was soon accompanied by a 600cc Silver Hawk. This had a narrow angle V-four engine with overhead camshaft and was obviously aimed at a more sporting public. It retained the Silver Arrow's spring frame and one-piece cylinder casting. At about this time Matchless took over the less fortunate A.J.S. under the new title of Associated Motor Cycles Ltd.

Prior to the Second World War, Matchless not only made their own motor cycles but also built and sold engines to other manufacturers like Brough Superior, Calthorpe and Morgan. During the war Matchless

350cc 63/L overhead valve single-cylinder machines were much in use by the British Army.

The post-war slump in the motor cycle industry did not cause Matchless to cease production. Their models included a 350cc and 500cc single-cylinder, and soon afterwards a complete range of motor cycles was available for the public from 250cc single to 650cc vertical twins. Post-war road racing successes were limited. The G.45, a 500cc push-rod twin racer never fulfilled its early promise, but the 500cc G.50, an overhead camshaft single-cylinder machine based on the 7R A.J.S., proved far more competitive with several seconds in the Senior T.T. The major post-war competitive success has been in trials and moto-cross. Associated Motor Cycles Ltd., took over other rivals who had fallen on hard times in the 1950s, such as James, Francis Barnett and Norton, enabling at least some of the marques to survive. The Collier brothers are remembered equally by enthusiasts for their racing successes and for their technical achievements – their motor cycles, the tri-car, the motor cycle and sidecar and the cycle-car. It is true to say that they were indeed Matchless.

31 MORGAN

H. F. S. Morgan designed and built his first three-wheeler in 1909 in a workshop attached to Malvern College, a well-known British public school. Initially it was constructed for his own personal use but within a year the first Morgan 'cyclecars' were available to the public.

The first Morgan consisted of two wheels and an engine at the front with chain-drive to the solitary rear wheel. There was a body similar to a car but with a single seat for the rider (or driver), on the outside of which there was a right-hand tiller for steering the vehicle. The brake and gear control levers were on the left allowing the driver (or rider) a choice of two speeds. The engine was a J.A.P. air-cooled single-cylinder capable of propelling the machine at a maximum speed of 50 m.p.h.

Three-wheelers were immensely popular in Britain before 1914 with over fifty different makes available. Whether the vehicle constituted a motor car or motor cycle was a much disputed matter and indeed to this day is a matter of opinion. Some three-wheelers were never designed along the lines of a motor cycle and fit comfortably into the motor car category. Those with engines of 1100cc or less and with a maximum vehicle weight of 7cwt, and which were also built on basic motor cycle principles, were classified as 'cyclecars' by the Auto Cycle Union and came under the A.C.U. umbrella for all purposes, including sporting competitions.

Since many of these three-wheelers were inspired by motor cycles rather than motor cars, it is correct to mention at least one make in an anthology of motor cycles. Most historians would agree that Morgans were the most popular and successful of the cyclecars for forty years.

The two-seater cyclecar provided a relatively cheap vehicle for the average married couple compared with motor cars or motor cycle combinations of the day (a pre-First World War Morgan cost under £90). It also provided a certain amount of weather protection with its optional hood and screen, a comparatively reliable engine and a ride which was not uncomfortable – or so the advertisers would have you believe!

A regular magazine was published for the enthusiast called 'The Cyclecar'. Since Morgan came into the field early and had imaginative leadership their machines soon took over as the most popular and successful cyclecar in trials and speed competitions. There was competition in this market from Continental manufacturers. Against such competition a Morgan took a gold medal in the London–Exeter trial of 1911 and won the 1913 Cyclecar Grand Prix in France. After the later success Morgan put a sporting Grand Prix Model into immediate production with a water-cooled V-twin overhead valve J.A.P. engine. By this time Morgan had outgrown the college workshop and were in manufacture at H.F.S. Morgan's newly acquired factory also in Malvern, Worcestershire. The vehicle itself had developed into a two-seater and the tiller control had long since been replaced by a steering wheel.

The major post-war development was the use of Swiss M.A.G. engines as well as the well-tried J.A.P. In the mid-twenties the Aero-Morgan, which superseded the Grand Prix as the sports model, was also available with Anzani or Blackburne engines. By this time the era of the cyclecar had passed and most rival manufacturers either ceased production or turned their whole attention to the mass manufacture of other small, cheap motor cars. For Morgan, however, sporting success at major trials and at Brooklands in speed competitions kept the interest in their particular three-wheeler alive and financially healthy. The factory was now under the general direction of George Goodall who maintained the high standard of Morgan machines by his enthusiasm and ability and encouraged even greater sporting achievements into the thirties.

Just before the Second World War a four-wheeler was put into production at the Morgan factory. Inevitably this signified the end of the cyclecar. At the conclusion of hostilities the factory continued to make the marvellous little three-wheeler but the popularity of the Morgan four-wheeler was such that in about 1950 it was decided to discontinue production of the former. In this way the Morgan cyclecar evolved into the Morgan motor car and so it continues to this day.

32 MOTO GUZZI

Como in Italy is not just famous for its beautiful lake. Among motor cyclists it is equally renowned as the home of perhaps the most popular Italian motor cycle, Moto Guzzi. The Guzzi factory (moto means 'motor, in Italian) was started in 1921 by Carlo Guzzi and has survived many world motor cycle market crises in the intervening years. In the 1920s Carlo Guzzi concentrated on the manufacture of 250cc and 500cc single-cylinder over-head valve and overhead camshaft models. Knowing the value of racing successes as advertisement for his standard road machines, Guzzi quickly entered into competitive road racing. Moto Guzzi were slightly unfor-tunate and shortsighted in their 1926 Isle of Man T.T. venture, when P. Ghersi rode his Guzzi into second place in the Lightweight race after recording the fastest lap speed, only to be disqualified on a remarkably small technicality – a switch of sparking plugs. The rule was that the machine parts during the races must be identical to the parts which had passed official scrutiny. One sparking plug difference seems a trifle to cause forfeiture of a winning place and could be seen as bad sportsmanship but for the fact that Moto Guzzi had prior warning of the risk they were running. They did not make that mistake again and the following year Archangli repeated the race success, this time without disqualification.

From the start Moto Guzzi have had a reputation in the 250cc class both for the standard product on sale to the public and for their racing models. From the earliest days of the factory the accent has been placed on pro-ducing lightweight machines which are fast and easy to handle. The enthusiasts are critical of their past inconsistency. This has certainly shown itself in road racing where a large number of retirements have prevented greater track success.

The Guzzi of the twenties was noted for its horizontal single-cylinder engine with the head facing forward to assist the air cooling. Even in those early days Guzzi combined the gearbox in unit with the crankcase. When certain marques like Matchless were going all out for the narrow angle Vee-cylinders, Guzzi took the opposite course with cylinders set at 120 degrees for their 500cc V-twin. They followed current trends with a low saddle position to improve the handling of their machines and also for streamlining purposes. Enthusiasts will remember that at a later date Guzzi set the trend with other streamlining devices.

Stanley Woods and Omobono Tenni were the works riders for Guzzi in the thirties who achieved great racing success, both claiming victories in the Lightweight T.T. races and Woods also in the Senior. Guzzi prospered in the pre-war years, but did not go under with the reversal of Italy's fortunes. Immediately following the Second World War, Guzzi bounced back with production of their Gambalunga (or 'long leg') 500cc single-cylinder machine designed specially for racing purposes. In Guzzi tradition it was light, a matter of 180 lbs, less than half the usual weight for a 500cc machine. Among its many noteworthy features was the pivoting fork rear suspension.

In post-war years the factory tended to specialise in the smaller production motor cycle and in this field they were very popular. The factory produced two- and four-stroke engines from 49cc to 250cc having particular success with their 98cc 'Zigolo' in the 1950s. In the larger class, the 1954 Guzzi Bialbero twin-camshaft racer and the V-8 water-cooled 500cc model brought out in 1957 for the factory team were regarded as rather special.

Their racing success was greatly assisted by riders of the calibre of Fergus Anderson, Ken Kavanagh and Bill Lomas who ensured victories and high placings in the T.T., Ulster and other Grands Prix of the fifties and sixties.

Moto Guzzi continues to thrive. Although Carlo Guzzi founded the company, the guiding influence for so many years were members of the Parodi family, Giorgio Parodi and Dr Angelo Parodi, who set the high standard of workmanship and skill in the pre-war years and created the internationally famous Moto Guzzi tradition.

The name of Moto Guzzi is now chiefly associated with mighty 750cc and 850cc transverse V-twins with shaft-drive although at the time of writing, 1973, there is talk of additional smaller models being on the way.

33 MOTOSACOCHE

The brothers Henri and Armand Dufaux may be regarded as pioneers of motor cycle progress. They commenced their business of manufacturing motor cycle engines at about the turn of the century in Geneva, Switzerland. They made their name in about 1905 with a development that was most acceptable to the 'man in the street' with little money to spend. The purchase of a motor cycle in those days in Britain cost as much as the equivalent of a year's wages. Their innovation was a power unit that could be attached to the ordinary pedal cycle and so transform it into a motorised cycle. The unit consisted of a double loop sub-frame of two parallel half-inch tubes, approximately 4 inches apart, into which the engine, magneto, petrol tank and belt pulley fitted snugly, giving rise to its name in French, 'moto' (motor or engine) 'sacoche' (tool bag or saddle bag), known in England as the 'Tool Bag Motor'.

This unit with its little four-stroke engine of $2\frac{1}{4}$ horsepower performed creditably in trials, and J. S. Holroyd's exploits in events of the 1908–9 period were quite amazing. He climbed gradients of 1 in 3, completing the course in many long distance trials with distinction and beating many machines of larger capacity.

The unit was manufactured under licence in many European countries and sold well in Great Britain. Several makers, notably Singer, fitted only this engine to their machines. But Motosacoche made other power units apart from their 'tool bag motor', and complete motor cycles as well. For this purpose another factory was opened in France at Lyon. Motosacoche products included single-cylinder and twin-cylinder models, and ranged from the small cycle attachment to a big 1,000cc overhead valve machine. Over the years many manufacturers used Motosacoche power units with the celebrated trademark of M.A.G., including the British firms Lea Francis, Brough Superior, Royal Enfield and Matchless. From 1910 until 1915 there was a particularly close connection with Royal Enfield and the two machines were almost identical.

Just before closing their motor cycle business in the early 1950s, Motosacoche once again caught the public eye with a special utility 200cc side valve model with belt-drive, which also incorporated the unusual brakeless front wheel, a creation of the designer Dougal Marchant, and his own fuel metering device making a carburettor unnecessary. Marchant had made his name with the sterling work put in on the 350cc overhead camshaft Chater-Lea in the 1920s both as designer and rider, and his performances on the Brooklands track are still remembered. The remarkable little Motosacoche was produced in the early post-war years, but gained insufficient support to prevent the directors from closing down the motor cycle department, while continuing the more flourishing business of making power units for industry. But the name Motosacoche is a reminder to all of the time when the firm had something rather special, all in the tool bag.

34 NORTON

In the minds of all motor cycling enthusiasts over the age of 15 the name 'Norton' is synonymous with racing. Like so many, Nortons have had financial crosses to bear, but in the world of motor cycle racing during the course of this century few other machines can claim such long term distinction and success.

In 1898 James Lansdowne (popularly better known later as 'Pa') Norton started up in business on his own to make parts for bicycles. He was 29 years of age and from his formative years had shown great interest in engineering. At the age of ten he was making working models of steam engines and later took an apprenticeship in engineering. The Norton Manufacturing Company produced its first motorised bicycle at Brace-bridge Street, Birmingham in 1902, with a $1\frac{1}{2}$ horsepower Clement Garard engine mounted on the front down tube. In the early years of Norton motor cycles, the continental engines produced by Clement, Moto-Reve and Peugeot were fitted, both single and twin with automatic inlet valves, and it was only after the success of the first ever T.T. win in 1907 that Pa Norton put his own engine in the motor cycle bearing his name. The Norton long-stroke 4 horsepower single known as the Big Four was introduced in that year and continued in production, with modifications, until 1954.

The Isle of Man Tourist Trophy was first run in 1907 and at first was more a test of the stamina of both machine and rider than speed (except in the changing of tyres or parts!). A Norton had the distinction of winning the twin-cylinder class of the first T.T., ridden by H. Rem Fowler, who entered the race as a private owner, with active assistance from Pa who was as enthusiastic as the rider. Rem Fowler won the class race on the only Norton in the field, but never actually received the winner's trophy of a silver rose bowl. The happy ending to that story is that in the late 1950s a T.T. 'Replica' trophy was donated by an erstwhile winner and before his death this was duly engraved and presented to the popular pioneer.

Norton started the T.T. races with success, and unlike any other manu-facturer can claim to have had entries in every T.T. meeting held.

By 1911 a 490cc engine was in production, the beginning of the models 16 and 16H which were popular with enthusiasts for so many years. Naturally enough Norton enetered the first Senior T.T. race run in that year.

In 1913 the Norton Manufacturing Co., was obliged to liquidate, but was re-constituted as Norton Motors Ltd. Under the guidance of Bill Mansell, production continued to provide a contribution to the war effort. Big Fours were sent to Russia, a tribute by the War Office to their well-known reliability. In 1919 chain-drive was introduced in place of the belt and three-speed Sturmey Archer gearboxes were fitted in an effort to improve performance.

The reputation of the Norton motor cycle was summed up in an advertising slogan 'the unapproachable Norton'. A delighted rider had written in gratitude that no other machine on the road could match his own. In later years, with the difficulties of mounting the specially prepared racing models with intricate streamlining, the slogan took on a new meaning! After the Great War came the great boom for motor cycles.

Reliability was still the all-important selling feature of any machine, but speed started to become a bigger factor: Nortons claimed both. A guarantee was issued with each $3\frac{1}{2}$ horsepower belt-driven model BS sold that it had been timed at Brooklands at 75 m.p.h. or more.

Overhead valves were introduced on Norton motor cycles in 1922, and with their arrival came the new mile record speed of 88·39 m.p.h. achieved by Rex Judd, a name closely associated with Nortons for many years. Without stalwarts such as Judd and particularly Mansell, Francis Beart, and Joe Craig with their manufacturing, design and tuning skills, the fame of Norton would have been far less. In the early 1920s the Maudes Trophy was awarded annually for quality in the standard production model of motor cycles. It might be possible to produce one machine out of a factory which could beat all competitors in a race, but this was of no use to the prospective purchaser unless the machine he was going to buy was of the same quality. A team of officials from the Auto Cycle Union deciding the award were given a demonstration of the general high standard of Norton in 1923. They were permitted to select individual parts at random in the factory to be assembled and mounted in a standard frame, which was run in for about eighty miles with minor adjustments and was then run continuously for twelve hours, during which time the speed averaged over 60 m.p.h. and eighteen world records were broken. When dismantled the engine was found to be in perfect condition. The award was instantly given to Norton, who won it for the next three years as well with a variety of stamina-proving tests, such as the journey from Lands End to John O' Groats and back (twice!) and 100 non-engine-stop ascents of Mount Snowden.

1924 was another landmark in the history of Norton, when Alec Bennett achieved Norton's first Senior victory in the T.T. races at an average of over 60 m.p.h. The Sidecar race was a walkover with more than half an hour separating the first two. Nortons also took first place in the French, Belgian and Spanish Grands Prix. Unhappily 'Pa' Norton died in 1925 leaving others to carry on the manufacturing of machines bearing his name. In the following year an overhead camshaft engine was introduced and with it came another Senior T.T. success.

Between 1931 and 1938 Nortons won every Senior and Junior T.T. race with two exceptions – a quite remarkable achievement. In the production field, the distinctive square-sided bevel box and offside magneto chain arrangement was introduced for 1930 on the overhead camshaft Norton. Other changes included a new lower frame with a shorter wheelbase and certain improvements in the front forks (such as rebound springs). Again a large contribution was made to the Second World War where some 25% of the solo or sidecar motor cycles used by British forces were made by Norton. But after the war only two 500cc models came off the production line: the side valve 16H and the overhead valve model 18, which was first introduced in the 1920s. Although girder forks were still fitted, the 'Roadholder' telescopic type, based on the ones used by the factory racers since 1938, were standardised soon afterwards.

Europe had been conquered by Nortons prior to the Second World War, but America was a new field. Between 1941 and 1953 Nortons won three times in the Daytona 100-mile race and five times in the 200-mile race with numerous 'place' successes.

In 1950 the firm put into production a new pivoted rear fork duplex frame. This was so much more comfortable for the rider than the former 'garden gate' design (with its plunger rear suspension) that it earned yet another nickname, which was to stick 'the Featherbed'. The Featherbed Norton, brainchild of the McCandless brothers, made a fairy story start in the 1950 T.T. races by taking the first three places in both Senior and Junior, and for the remainder of that decade Nortons made the greatest impression of any make upon the road racing scene.

Norton's Diamond Jubilee in 1958 saw the introduction of the first baby Norton, a 250cc machine, but the end of the Bracebridge Street reign was nigh. In 1962 Norton's were taken over by Associated Motorcycles Ltd., and moved down to London premises. A.M.C. in turn ceased to exist and the name passed to Norton Villiers Ltd. Production continues and perhaps great success lies ahead, but it is unlikely that Norton could now improve on its past record of achievement.

Some of the famous racing riders closely associated with Nortons were Alec Bennett, Jimmy Simpson, Stanley Woods and Jim Guthrie in the 1920s and 1930s. Then Geoff Duke, Ray Amm, Bob McIntyre and Eric Oliver starred in the 1950s, and more recently John Surtees, and Mike Hailwood (who won the 1961 T.T. averaging over 100 m.p.h. on a single-cylinder Norton), Phil Read and Peter Williams. People who know nothing of motor cycle racing are familiar with those names, and even people who know nothing of motor cycles are familiar with the name Norton.

35 N.S.U.

The German name N.S.U. is perhaps best known for its lightweight models and mopeds, which became so popular in the 1950–1965 period before the Japanese made inroads in this field. But the factory at Neckarsulm has been manufacturing motor cycles now for over seventy years, and was originally noted for its V-twins of 500cc, 750cc and 1,000cc. Founded in 1901, the Neckarsulmer Fahrzeugwerke at first used Minerva or Sedel (ZL) engines but it was not long before their own engines were in production. A distinctive feature of the early years was the N.S.U. two-speed epicyclic gear combined with the engine pulley. This successfully overcame the gear problem created by belt-drive encountered by all pioneer motor cycle engineers. As with other gear devices, the consequence was rapid belt wear and frequent replacement. However, subsequent modifications made the gear one of the most popular throughout Europe, and the component was purchased separately by many motor cycle entusiasts for adaption to their own British machines. It was listed as a factory extra by several manufacturers, notably Bradbury.

Prior to the First World War imported products were not much in demand as there were a number of good quality British motor cycles on the market. However the N.S.U. with its coil springing, was perhaps one of the most popular foreign-made motor cycles. N.S.U. continued to produce V-twin models until the mid-twenties and thereafter concentrated on their new unit construction singles of both side valve and overhead valve in a range of 500cc and below.

It was not until after the Second World War that N.S.U. started to make their very popular lightweight motor cycles and mopeds. The range commenced with the 100cc and 250cc models and subsequently varied between 49cc and 300cc. The N.S.U. 49cc model became very popular in Britain with young persons of both sexes; apart from its inexpensive running costs and minimal weight, it still had a surprising turn of speed. It was a single-cylinder air-cooled two-stroke machine with two- or three-speed gearbox. The 98cc Fox and 247cc Max with overhead camshaft single-cylinder engines were equally popular among persons of all ages.

In the 1950s the factory concentrated much time and money on making successful racing machines and dominated the 125cc and 250cc classes for a few years. They also took the 'world's fastest' with a 'blown' 500cc twin, and added a large number of world records in the 50cc to 500cc classes to their list of achievements. During this time the factory took a batch of machines to Daytona in the USA for world record attempts, and were so confident that the reporting journalists were given typed lists of the existing records to be attacked with spaces left for insertion of the new date and speed to be achieved by the N.S.U. machine! The confidence proved well-founded as N.S.U. took every record attempted.

At the present time the name of N.S.U. is associated mainly with motor cars although the two-wheelers are still produced under licence in countries other than Germany.

The three letters N.U.T., while striking an appropriately mechanical note, were in fact not adopted by the makers of the motor cycle for that reason, but were the initials of the home town of the factory, Newcastle-upon-Tyne. For those readers unfamiliar with Britain, Newcastle-upon-Tyne is set in the heart of the industrial North-East of England, which is perhaps more noted for its beer and football team than for the subject of this history.

The N.U.T. must be one of the least-known makes of motor cycle to have won a T.T. race in the Isle of Man. This victory was recorded in the 1913 Junior T.T. with Hugh Mason in the saddle. Hugh Mason was almost a 'one-man-band' at N.U.T. since he was not only the machine's designer, but also chief test rider and racer. By 1913 many of the big names in motor cycle manufacturing dominated the racing scene, as victories were viewed as the best advertisement for the product. Victory in the T.T. was the highest achievement of all in those days, as it demonstrated a machine's reliability as well as speed over the two hundred miles of its course. Success there meant an immediate increase in sales. The Junior race won by Mason was over a shorter course than the Senior event, but still covered 225 miles of rough roads unlike the tarmacadam in the Island today. Greater credit than ever must therefore be accorded to Mason for his victory in view of the competition he fended off from bigger rival companies. The N.U.T. factory had only been started a couple of years before, and was at this date a very small organisation making a handful of machines a month. Mason and his J.A.P.-engined 350cc twin-cylinder machine recorded the fastest lap speed of the race at over 45 m.p.h., and maintained an average over the whole race of 43·75 m.p.h. to win by just under a minute from his nearest rival, W. F. Newsome on a Douglas. But Mason's victory was no flash in the pan. A warning had been given by the firm's first attempt in the T.T. races the year before, when R. W. Ellis riding the only N.U.T. entry came into a very creditable sixth place, also in the Junior race.

In the three years before the First World War the very few N.U.T. entries in the T.T. races all managed to bring credit to the makers (with the exception of a couple of retirements) but none could equal Mason's achievement of 1913. N.U.T. never entered road racing to the same extent after the war and public interest in the marque waned. Enforced interruption of manufacture caused by the 1914–18 war may have affected the progress and development of the N.U.T. motor cycle. Like so many factories in Britain, the N.U.T. engineering facilities were involved in more important war work and motor cycle production ceased until 1919. A last T.T. fling in 1914 saw N.U.T. in both Senior and Junior races, and with the Spaniard, S. Sorriquieta, riding in both, much was hoped for in the northerners' camp. However, 11th place was the best he could do in the Junior and he failed to finish in the 500cc race.

After the war the factory continued motor cycle production where it had left off, now building their own engines. The machine still had its distinctive low frame, with round tank secured by metal straps in the splendid brown finish. An amusing advertising campaign showed a poster-size walnut to catch public attention. The biggest change came in the next two or three years when Hugh Mason, the architect of N.U.T., severed all connections with the firm.

In the post-war years the majority of the firm's machines were powered by home-produced N.U.T. engines, and the models ranged from the 350cc machine, which had represented the manufacturers so well over the years, up to the 1000cc. Nearly all the models were powered by twin-cylinder engines. N.U.T. had earlier experimented with several engine makes, but generally settled for the reliable J.A.P. The emphasis at N.U.T. was always on quality before utility, and with the quality came expensive prices, such as the 140-guinea tag attached to their 1920 model. The high purchase price did not help sales. Prices were steadily reduced each year for the basic model but the competition was too great, despite the quality offered. In the late 1920s, when unemployment and poverty were the rule rather than the exception, the knowledge that he received good value for money did not help the prospective buyer to find the necessary cash to buy an N.U.T. The price of the product together with internal disputes at the factory and the national crisis combined to ensure that N.U.T. ceased production by the early 1930s – leaving the reputation of Newcastle-upon-Tyne to be maintained solely by the footballers and brewers of that town.

37 P AND M

In 1900 Joah Carver Phelon set to work on the construction of a motor cycle. While others were finding great difficulty in deciding where to put the engine, he made up his mind right away. He removed the front down tube from a cycle frame and inserted the engine in its place, with direct chain-drive to the rear wheel – a far-sighted decision in the days of almost universal belt drive. Harry Rayner was joint patentee of the frame design and his influence was considerable in the machine's development until his untimely death in 1903.

A few machines were made, but since resources were so limited, the design was offered to Humber, who were well established at that time with a vast output of pedal cycles. An arrangement to pay a royalty of 7s. 6d. per machine to Mr Phelon was made. The sloping engine 'Humber' was popular during 1902–3 after which time a fresh model was planned. An associate of Phelon's named Moore realised the potential of the design with a new two-speed gear, and persuaded him to retrieve the licence.

With this fresh venture the Phelon and Moore partnership came into being in May 1904. Their machine had the same sloping engine mounting, two-speed gear and 'free' engine (obtained by two primary chains from the engine sprockets with expanding clutches). This placed the model well ahead of rivals with fixed belt-drive, which necessitated a run-and-bump start after every stop.

A basic change to mechanical inlet valves was made in 1910, all previous machines having had automatic inlet valves. Certain other detail improvements were also made, but the two-speed gear was retained. This enabled the firm to take an interest in competitions, chiefly in reliability trials where these well-made machines excelled. Many successes were also obtained in long-distance events and the A.C.U. Quarterly Trials. The smartness of the models and their riders was a special feature of this period. Attention to appearance was noted by the onlookers, a custom not observed by the majority of riders whose bikes showed the stain of travel on dusty roads.

When war broke out and the Royal Flying Corps was formed the P and M was adopted as the official despatch riders' machine of the Corps, and gave excellent service.

During the twenties racing interests culminated in a creditable 4th place in the Senior T.T. of 1925, with rider T. F. Bullus. Subsequent appearances in the T.T. gave them 10th place in the Senior of 1927 and 9th the following year.

The name Panther had been added to the P and M when up-dating the range in 1926, together with the introduction of saddle tanks.

In 1927 a totally different model was introduced into the range, having an engine-gearbox unit designed by Granville Bradshaw. This little machine, the Panthette, had a 250cc o.h.v. V-twin engine set across the frame. Its unusual construction included a forged channel-type frame and four-speed gearbox which transmitted power to the rear wheel by chain.

The small engine was not a success and production was dropped after two years. In this period the 500cc models had been developed with overhead valves and four-speed gearboxes, again ahead of most rivals, while in 1928 the first of the famous 600s was offered for sidecar work. With modifications this machine was produced until the close-down of the factory.

The depression in 1930 caused much concern with manufacturers and many dropped prices to maintain sales, offering inferior products. P and M continued to offer a quality machine, but the notorious 'Red' Panther, a healthy 250, sold readily at £29 17s. 6d. under the banner of Pride and Clarke, the South London dealers.

Many models were offered from time to time – even a two-stroke powered by a 250 Villiers engine – but the mainstay was the 600cc model. It is a tribute to Phelon's design that his first machine of 1900 should have the engine replacing the front down tube, and that the last one, manufactured sixty-six years later, retained this basic feature.

38 ROYAL ENFIELD

Royal Enfield must be regarded as one of the foremost British motor cycles ever made. The Enfield Cycle Company produced their first motor bicycle at the turn of the century and their last in the mid-sixties, and in between earned a proud reputation for quality and reliability. Motor cycles of various cubic capacities were manufactured during this time under the name of Royal Enfield, but it is perhaps in the lightweight division of 350cc and below that they are best remembered and achieved their greatest success.

An interest in engineering led the Redditch-based company under the guiding influence of Robert Walker Smith to the manufacture of cycles and cycle parts in the 1890s. The natural progress from there was to bring mechanisation to these machines, like so many of their rivals in the Midlands. The first of the Enfield motorised cycles was in fact a quadricycle made in about 1898, and quadricycles and tricycles with de Dion engines were manufactured and sold by the company for several years. Early experiments with two-wheeled machines led to the production of a motor bicycle in 1901, with a small clip-on engine fixed in front of the steering column which drove the rear wheel by means of an elongated crossed belt. The machine was also fitted with pedals for supplementary human drive! The position of the engine was soon changed for later models to the conventional place below the petrol tank. Early Enfields were of $2\frac{3}{4}$ horsepower and $3\frac{1}{2}$ horsepower. During the first decade interest at Enfield had naturally extended to experiments with motorcars and a subsidiary company was soon established for their manufacture.

From the outset the name, symbol and trade-mark of the Royal Enfield motor cycle displayed the firm's close business association with the Royal Small Arms Factory in Enfield, Middlesex. The symbol showed a field gun with the words 'Royal Enfield' pierced by a rifle with bayonet fixed. Early

Enfield colours were two shades of green which persisted throughout their range of models until the late twenties.

By 1910 the company had transferred their allegiance to miniature V-twins of about 350cc based loosely on the Swiss-made Motosacoche design. They developed an expanding clutch two-speed gear similar to that used by the P and M and Scott motor cycles, which involved twin primary chains. The big innovation of the pre-First World War years was the 6 horsepower twin-cylinder model with a passenger chair powered by a J.A.P. engine, an interesting contrast to the MAG 8 horsepower twin used by Matchless. However, the J.A.P. engine was an exception in the house of Enfield, where until the war the connection with Motosacoche had been very marked although not publicised. The range of Motosacoche twins sold in England had components of considerable similarity to Enfield's, including the rubber 'cush' hub in the rear wheel to take the punch out of the chain-drive, a feature that was to be incorporated into all Royal Enfield motor cycles until the very end. In the immediate post-war years the Royal Enfield passenger outfits were powered by Vickers and Wolseley 8 horse-power twins. From those early days Enfield's continued to cater for the sidecar enthusiast. In the twenties the 1000cc J.A.P. twin was superseded by Enfield's own engine, and then supplemented by a 1140cc side valve unit in the thirties. Post-Second World War sidecar models included the 500cc o.h.v. single-cylinder Model J, followed by the 700cc 'Meteor' in the mid-fifties, which was the first of the big parallel overhead valve twins.

The year 1914 marked Enfield's first really successful venture in the Isle of Man T.T. Races. From the earliest days Royal Enfield entered trials and road reliability tests without disgrace, competing as early as 1900 in the 1,000 Miles Trial with their quadricycle, but in the world of racing the marque never, so to speak, made its mark. In the 1914 Junior T.T. however, eight out of nine Royal Enfields finished, with a very creditable five in the first twenty places. The best performance of the day for Enfield ended in tragedy. F. J. Walker was in contention for first place when he crashed on the last lap. Picking his machine up, undoubtedly in great pain, he managed to start his machine again and crossed the finishing line in third place following home the two Williams on their A.J.S. machines. Whether due to concussion suffered in the crash, or for some other unknown reason, he continued to ride down the road and collided fatally with the barriers, which in those days were placed across the road at the conclusion of the race. Post-war racing success for Royal Enfield was mainly confined to the twenties, the Company thereafter preferring to give their support to entries in trials competitions. In the twenties C. S. Barrow rode Enfields with considerable racing success, and among other trophies he helped them to win was the team award in the 1927 Junior T.T. event. The following year

Barrow attained his personal best in T.T. races with a second place on his Enfield in the Lightweight class, coming in behind F. A. Longman on his O.K. Supreme.

For trials the company made the well-loved range of 'Bullet' models starting in the early 1930s. These were light machines usually driven by a 350cc engine. After the Second World War the 'Bullet' was one of the pioneers of the swinging arm rear suspension that is now in universal use, and 350 and 500cc 'Bullets' had a staunch following for many years. The 'Meteor' of the mid-fifties was basically a pair of 350cc Bullets placed side by side. Other innovations of the thirties in the Royal Enfield factory included the 'Cycar' model, a 150cc two-stroke machine, remarkable for its completely enclosed frame and engine and low purchase price of about £20. When it is remembered that the first Royal Enfield cost in the region of £50, this was an advance appreciated by all Enfield enthusiasts. In the sporting field, trials successes were recorded for Royal Enfield in the decade before the Second World War by men like Holdsworth and Booker and the legendary Charlie Rogers.

Royal Enfield's contribution to the war effort of 1939–45 included the supply of 350cc overhead valve models for British dispatch riders (based on their highly successful trials model) and the 'Flying Flea' models, so called because of their compact size and their special purpose. These 125cc two-stroke machines together with the Excelsior-made 'Corgi' provided instant transport for the Allied paratroop divisions landed in Europe. The design of the 'Flying Flea' bore remarkable similarities to the German D.K.W. equivalent and appeared to many people to be a blatant copy. However, as far as Enfields were concerned, they filled a need and continued the factory's history of two-strokes which had begun in 1915. The 'Flea' developed later into the 'Prince' model but this died a natural death.

In the early fifties, apart from the Bullet range, Enfield's most notable contribution was the big parallel twin 'Meteor' mentioned earlier. In the smaller cubic capacity range, Enfield's 250cc 'Clipper' was quite popular. In the later part of the decade another 250cc model, the unit construction 'Crusader', was launched, with a performance better than the same capacity German N.S.U. It was a bold and brave venture, halted mainly by the dying public interest in British-made motor cycles.

Certainly after the war Enfields had continued to prove themselves in trials' competitions, their most successful exponent being Johnny Brittain, but continental two-strokes followed by the Japanese challenge hit the British industry very hard. In a final fling, Enfield's showed a surprising renewed interest in road racing with a 250cc two-stroke single-cylinder machine with great potential. It might well have proved a winner with a little more development. But 'the might-have-beens' litter the world of motor cycling history and for Royal Enfield the history book closed in the mid-sixties when all production ceased.

Thereafter Enfield owners requiring spare parts obtained them from Velocette, until they too ceased production in 1971.

39 RUDGE

Rudge were in the transport business as early as the 1870s, when Dan Rudge made a popular pedal cycle. Rudge started and ended as manufacturers of pedal cycles, sandwiching a thirty-year period of manufacturing very good motor cycles. Dan Rudge hailed from the Midlands, as did the Coventry-born man named Woodcock, initially a lawyer, who took over Rudge and several other cycle companies at the turn of the century to house them all under one roof and the one name of Rudge. After he died the Rudge company joined forces with the Whitworth cycle company of Birmingham to become Rudge Whitworth. The power behind the new company was Charles Pugh, who had been a top man at Whitworth's prior to the merger.

The first Rudge-Whitworth motor cycle was manufactured at their Coventry-based works in 1910. There was nothing remarkable in the design. It had a 499cc single-cylinder engine with the unusual feature of a push-rod operated overhead inlet valve. Like its contemporaries, it used direct belt-drive. However in 1911 the factory introduced a new gear system for machines to be ridden in the Isle of Man T.T. races, which was subsequently incorporated in their standard model on sale to the public. It was known as the Multi gear and, like the Gradua gear designed by Freddie Barnes for Zenith, it provided a variable gear while retaining the smoothness and simplicity of belt-drive. The gear was operated alongside the petrol tank by a lever which opened or closed the engine and rear wheel pulleys together, but in different directions, so that the belt tension was kept constant. By this method an infinitely variable gear could be obtained, over a fairly limited range. The wear and tear on the belt was such that replacements were constantly needed. The gear became both popular and successful and Rudge-Whitworth motor cycles which included this particular gear were known as Rudge-Multis.

Rudges were first entered for the T.T. races in 1912, and their first victory came with Cyril Pullin on his 500cc single-cylinder Rudge-Multi in the 1914 Senior T.T., improving on Ray Abbott's second in the preceding year's event. Pullin recorded a remarkably good race average of 49·5 m.p.h. Cyril Pullin himself re-designed the Rudge-Multi for racing by the inclusion of a long steering head and sloping top tube, making the petrol tank a wedge shape and generally improving the machine's handling.

The new V-twin for 1915 was called the Multwin and still incorporated belt-drive with the ever popular multi-gear. Surprisingly it was also offered with the alternative of a new countershaft three-speed gearbox.

Like other top manufacturers Rudge made motor cycles for the First World War and a large proportion of their output found its way to the Russian front.

Rudge continued to produce their 'Multi' model until the mid-twenties but thereafter only two models were put on the market. These were powered by single-cylinder 499cc and 349cc engines with pent-roof four valve cylinder heads, and incorporated four-speed gearboxes and coupled brakes. The all-black tank was now picked out with gold lines, and the full Rudge-Whitworth name appeared where only the abbreviated version had been seen before. The range was extended later to include 500cc four valve machines in 'Standard', 'Special' and 'Sports' models. Bulbous saddle tanks were a distinctive feature of the Special and Sports models. For 1929 the Sports model was re-named the 'Ulster' in commemoration of Graham Walker's success in the Grand Prix of 1928, the first road race in the world to be won at an average speed of over 80 m.p.h. In the same year Rudge-Whitworth put out their first lightweight 250cc side valve and overhead valve motor cycles, engines courtesy of J.A.P. For 1931 they built their own 250cc overhead valve engine with four valves, which proved very successful in T.T. racing in the 1930s.

The new decade saw the introduction of dry sump lubrication and a new design of the crankcase on the four valve models.

In keeping with the popular trend, the black petrol tank was replaced by a chromium tank with black panels. The new 1930 Rudge could reach 100 m.p.h., or so it was claimed. Certainly it beat all its contemporaries on the T.T. course, taking first, second and fourth in the Senior and first and second in the Junior. Walter Handley, who won the Senior, had intended to ride an F.N. which failed to arrive in time for the race, and so he 'borrowed' a Rudge. Rudges had many successes in the T.T. races of the 1930s, notably in the hands of those most able riders Graham Walker, Ernie Nott, H. G. Tyrell-Smith, Charlie Dodson and Walter Handley. After the Senior-Junior double of 1930, success was limited to the Lightweight class where they eventually achieved first, second and third in 1934. Rudge-Whitworth were also successful in many trials including the Blue Ribbon event, the International Six Days.

In 1938 the factory moved to Hayes in Middlesex. Two years later the company sold out to Sturmey Archer and Norman Motor Cycles and the name Rudge-Whitworth passed into the history books of motor cycling.

40 SCOTT

Alfred Angas Scott, a dyer's technician from Yorkshire, developed twin two-stroke engines to propel bicycles and later his motor boat. By 1908 these experiments bore fruit in the production of the first Scott motor cycle. Like so many pioneers, Alfred Scott had to overcome lack of finance and this was temporarily achieved by allowing another engineering concern to build and sell the machines to his design. He received the handsome royalty of £3 10s 0d (£3.50) on each motor cycle made. The first Scott's were powered by a small parallel twin two-stroke engine, with deflector-type pistons and water-cooled cylinder heads slung extremely low in a wide duplex cradle frame. The straight tube of the frame gave it the appearance of a ladies' bicycle. The duplex-tubed open frames favoured by Scott were reminiscent of those first used in the early experiments of the Hildebrand brothers in Germany in the 1890s. The Scott motor cycle had a rear wheel drive via two chains to a countershaft and a single chain for the final drive.

In 1909, Scott, together with his cousin Frank Philipp and another enthusiast Eric Myers, organised their own Bradford factory for production of Scott motor cycles, backed partly by money from Scott's brothers. Even so it was uneconomic to manufacture frames, and these were supplied by Royal Enfield to Scott's specifications and design. Early advances made by Alfred Scott included internal enclosed spring front forks (forerunners of the telescopic forks of today) the kick-starter, the foot-change two-speed gear pedal, and all-chain-drive.

Scott's were unusual for being two-strokes at a time when most motor cycles were four-strokes. They were renowned for their quiet engines, fast acceleration, low centre of gravity and their lightness and ease of handling. From the very beginning, Alfred Scott had caused jealousy among rival manufacturers, and when in 1908 he had swept the board with three gold medals in an important hill climbing event, there were complaints that on a two-stroke machine he had an unfair advantage over the other competitors. The Auto Cycle Union ordered him to alter his engine to deprive himself of the advantage. In time this apparently absurd penalty was removed. However, it did not interfere with Scott's plans for the Isle of Man Senior Tourist Trophy Races, and in 1912 Frank Applebee rode his Scott to victory in the Senior T.T., recording an average speed over the 187½-mile course of 48·69 miles per hour. In the 1913 Senior T.T. this Scott success was repeated by H. O. Wood. In 1912 business had improved and another factory was opened, this time in nearby Shipley, Yorkshire. Success in the Isle of Man T.T. was guaranteed to boost sales.

For the First World War Scott developed a sidecar-outfit-style, shaft-drive 'gun-car'. Soon after the war Alfred Scott with his colleagues decided to sell their interest in Scott motor cycles. Scott considered he had made as much progress in the development of the two-wheeler as he could hope to make in the foreseeable future, and felt he could more usefully apply his talents to the manufacture of a unique side-car combination, the 'Sociable'. With his departure went some of the inspiration behind the progress of Scott's, and despite the comparative success of the Squirrel series and the boom in popularity at the end of the twenties, Scott's were never pacemakers in motor cycling again.

The Squirrel series started in 1922 with a sports model of 486cc with light mudguards and dropped handlebars. H. Langman boosted the Scott 'Squirrel' with a third in the Senior T.T. and Scott's also took the Team Prize, finishing in fourth and ninth places.

By 1925 the 'Super Squirrel' was on the scene in 498cc and 596cc forms with water-cooled cylinder heads. The 596cc was specially built with sidecars in mind. In 1926 Scott produced their 'Flying Squirrel', a newly tuned twin watercooled two-stroke, still on the duplex open frame with the optional extra of the elongated tank used on their T.T. machines.

In the thirties there was a significant change from the duplex frame to a frame with a single down tube. The detachable cylinder head was introduced and the short-stroke engine was retired. The Scott factory also made a three-cylinder water-cooled luxury machine. Like many British motor cycle manufacturers, financial clouds continuously hovered on the horizon and the Second World War added greatly to Scott's difficulties. Soon after the war in 1950, Matthew Holder's Aerco Jig and Tool factory in Birmingham bought Scott's and from that time on, under new management, Scott motor cycles were built to order in Birmingham. But for all the various hands that have controlled the destiny of Scott motor cycles, the touch of Alfred Angas Scott is still very much in evidence to this day, since the design of his original motor cycle remained basically unchanged through some sixty years.

41 SINGER

Singer and Company of Coventry drew considerable attention with the 'motor wheel' used to propel their motor bicycles and tricycles at the turn of the century. Messrs. Perks and Birch, also of Coventry, patented the device in 1899. The 'motor wheel' was a wheel with engine, petrol tank and complete motorising works within its perimeter, which could be fitted to a perfectly ordinary pedal bicycle or tricycle. Perks and Birch were intending to put their invention out to the public under the appropriate name of the 'Compact', but in 1900 Singer put the machine on the market with a 2 horsepower four-stroke engine mounted in the middle of an aluminium spoked wheel. The 'motor wheel' was usually the rear wheel in the bicycle and the front wheel of the tricycle. It was probably the first motor cycle fitted with a magneto, a low tension type with make and break inside the combustion chamber, for which the credit must go to F. R. Simms. The speed of the machine was controlled by a lever which operated by a form of throttle control to the carburettor. The 'motor wheel' proved very popular indeed in the first few years of the century and Singer earned a reputation, despite the obvious awkward positioning of the petrol tank and the engine. By 1904 the wheel was re-designed with the spokes of the wheel all placed on one side to improve access. Singer also catered for the lady rider with their dropped frame model. Both ladies and men were given the opportunity to assist their motorised cycles with pedalling equipment, a common feature of nearly all motor cycles at the beginning of the century.

After 1904 Singer motor cycles were re-designed. A central vertical engine was fitted between a split front down tube of the cycle frame, and the machine was fitted with a new high tension magneto fixed in front of the engine, protected from the grit and grime by the valanced front mudguard.

It was not long before Singer were experimenting with a three-wheeler (as opposed to the tricycle which had always been popular with them). From there it was but a short step to the four-wheel motor car. The Singer car was available by the end of the first decade of the century, and motor cars eventually dominated motor cycle production in the Company.

Singer's always made their own engines and after the 'motor wheel' produced both two-stroke and four-stroke machines, the early models being air-cooled and the later models water-cooled. One of their most popular machines just prior to the First World War was the 500cc four-stroke single-cylinder model. This model was often used with sidecars, enabling the enthusiast to be accompanied by a fellow enthusiast or even his wife! Never a great success in racing competitions (fifth in the 1913 Junior T.T. was the high spot in their short career) and at first disdaining to enter trials (such as the first Auto Cycle Club 1,000-miles Trial in 1903), Singer's were undoubtedly popular with the 'everyday' motor cyclist. However, the company's decision to concentrate on motor car production meant the end of the motor cycle department in 1915. It was a short but illustrious life that made a worthwhile contribution to the development of motor cycles.

John Marston and Co. were an old-established Midlands firm which manufactured saucepans and other metal items until they turned their attention
to bicycles in 1890. They were immediately successful in this venture.
In 1912 their first motor cycle was produced almost entirely in their works,
and was a neat little $2\frac{3}{4}$ horsepower (350cc) side valve machine with a two-
speed gearbox and an attractively painted green tank with silver panels. As
the quality was high, so was the price and only a few were sold. In 1913,
in addition to the $2\frac{3}{4}$ (now fitted with the famous black tank with gold
line) a $3\frac{1}{2}$ horsepower single and 6 horsepower J.A.P.-engined twin were
offered principally for sidecar use. Unfortunately, the 500cc machine
had many teething troubles, resulting in a redesigned engine for 1915, when
military orders were secured from the French and Russian governments.
Since both preferred final belt-drive, the only belt-drive machines made by
this firm were produced. All the $3\frac{1}{2}$ horsepower machines had three-speed
countershaft gearboxes, and all civilian models primary and final drive in
oil bath chain cases. The V-twin machine was powered by various engines
including the Swiss M.A.G., but from 1917 until 1923 the 8 horsepower
J.A.P. was fitted.

After the war modification and improvements were made to the $3\frac{1}{2}$ horsepower model, but the $2\frac{3}{4}$ horsepower machine was discontinued. The
decision to re-enter racing to back up the considerable success already
achieved in reliability trials was taken as soon as events were organised.
In 1920 T. C. De La Hay had a handsome victory in the Senior T.T.
race in the Isle of Man. Two years later Alec Bennett scored another victory
for the marque in the same event. They were obliged to wait until 1928
for Charlie Dodson to win another Senior T.T. for them, but he repeated
the performance the following year with Alec Bennett pursuing him home
in second place. Sunbeams were not to experience T.T. success like this
again.

In the mid-twenties an overhead camshaft engine of 600cc was designed
with a view to competing in the sidecar T.T. races, but this was never used
and an experimental 500cc version proved equally unsuccessful.

In the thirties Sunbeam standard models with 250, 350, 500 and 600cc
side valve and overhead valve single-cylinder engines were marketed with
moderate success. Any lack of success can be attributed fairly to the high
purchase price, beyond the reach of so many purses. The make retained
such a reputation for quality and handsome finish through its entire production, that it was often referred to as the gentleman's motor cycle.

John Marston's were taken over in 1937 by Associated Motor Cycles and the design continued as before until the war. After hostilities the name Sunbeam passed to the B.S.A. Group, and was used on an entirely new range of luxury mount models the S.7 and S.8. These were notable for their huge tyres and overhead camshaft vertical twin engines with shaft-drive, the frames being fully sprung. Unhappily these did not prove a financial success and were discontinued in the mid-fifties. The final appearance of the name was on the ill-fated B.S.A. groups scooter. A sad end to a famous British marque.

43 SUZUKI

Suzuki is now probably one of the most popular makes of motor cycle in the world. But it was not until the mid-fifties that this Japanese company even considered making such machines, having previously made its name and money on specialised engineering directed at the textile trade. The company was founded in 1909 by Michio Suzuki and the first factory was opened for production at Hamamatsu. In 1952, following a drastic recession in textiles, the company looked for another outlet for their engineering knowledge, experience and craftsmen. It was quite a step to enter the world of motor cycle production.

In 1953 the first Suzuki motor cycle was produced in Japan and like all that were to follow, it was a two-stroke. At the time of deciding company policy, the two-stroke machine was not considered by most manufacturers to be a profitable or worthwhile field, but like other Japanese manufacturers, Suzuki proved the fallacy of this theory. The first ever Suzuki motor cycle was a 60cc model and so great an impact did it make, that production was almost immediately increased to a remarkable 4,400 power units per month, approximately equivalent to the total number of power units produced by all the British manufacturers at that point in time.

In 1954 the company changed its name to Suzuki Motor Company Ltd. 1955 saw the first Suzuki 125cc and at the same time Suzuki produced their first Mini motor car, again powered by a two-stroke engine. With the increasing demand for their motor cycles, the company expanded gradually over the years until at the time of writing there are five factories set up in Japan concentrating on production of Suzuki machines. Suzuki in fact manufacture boats and outboard motors for boats, and Snowcats which are better known in colder climates where mobility is still required even when the snow lies thickly upon the ground.

The range of Suzuki motor cycles has also increased over the years and there is now available to the enthusiast a choice of any size machine from the 50cc single cylinder five-speed gearbox model up to the 750cc water cooled three cylinder Super Bike, all two-stroke machines. Suzuki can fairly be described as the motor cycle of today and tomorrow, and their 'history' is still to be made. The company have, however, in the few short years of their motor cycling existence managed to stake a claim to fame in both 'tourist' and 'competition' worlds. Suzuki have always aimed at making their machines attractive to the prospective purchaser, the man in the street, and have placed the emphasis on the facility of starting, the smooth running of the engine, the comfortable seats, bright paintwork and chrome. But pretty colours alone do not sell motor cycles, and the true credit for the success of Suzuki must rest with the engineers. Even now with an eye to the future and the ever increasing world wide pollution problem, Suzuki have obtained the world manufacturing rights for the production of the re-volutionary Wankel rotory engine. This, however, is still in the future.

Suzuki sales since production began have been remarkable, and have been particularly high in the USA. In Great Britain the Suzuki franchise came under the management of the Lambretta/Trojan Group and established themselves firmly in the market.

Suzuki have also had considerable success in motor cycle competition, be it racing or trials. The factory's first entry in the Isle of Man T.T. races was in 1960 but it was not until the innovation of the 50cc event that Suzuki had their first T.T. success. Suzuki had the distinction of being the first winners of the 50cc T.T. race in 1962, Ernst Degner managing to average over 75 m.p.h. round the $75\frac{1}{2}$ mile course, a quite astonishing performance. Suzuki emphasised its superiority in this class by winning again in 1963 and 1964. 1963 was indeed a successful T.T. year for Suzuki as the factory took the coveted 1, 2, 3 placings in the Lightweight 125cc event in addition to the 50cc trophy. Road racing success has continued since that time with much credit due to riders like Hugh Anderson and Barry Sheene. Other notable racing successes have been achieved in moto-cross grands prix and in 1971 their riders won all four of the manufacturers and individuals titles in the 250cc and 500cc events giving them complete victory in the 1971 World Moto-cross Grand Prix. In 1972 they again won the 250cc and 500cc world championships.

It is small wonder that the name Suzuki is associated the world over more with motor cycles than with engineering in the textile industry. For Suzuki motor cycles, the story is only just beginning.

44 TRIUMPH

The founder of the Triumph pedal cycle business chose a name that was easily identifiable on the continent as in Britain, since he himself was a German living in London, Siegfried Bettmann. The cycle business was started in 1885 and Bettmann soon joined forces with another German, Schulte at their Coventry premises in the midland area of England. In 1897 the 'New Triumph Cycle Co., Ltd.', was formed but the title was soon shortened. Schulte, the chief engineer, was naturally interested in the new developments in engine-propelled bicycles and in the German-made Hildebrand and Wolfmuller. But Triumph did not rush into a venture ill-prepared. It was not until 1902 that the world saw the first Triumph motor cycle. This was a single-geared, single-cylinder motor bicycle, with a Minerva engine fitted below the front down tube of the frame and with the petrol tank clipped to the crossbar. This was followed by a similar machine with a J.A.P. engine in 1903. Schulte introduced the first Triumph motor cycle engine in 1905 and it soon gained popularity. In the first Isle of Man Tourist Trophy events, Triumphs came second and third in the single-cylinder class, and improved on that performance the following year by winning the event with Jack Marshall in the saddle. Triumph motor cycles featured high in the honours list of motor cycle sporting competitions from the start. Triumph's designed their own carburettor and fitted magneto ignition to improve the reliability of their $3\frac{1}{2}$ horsepower machine in performance, so much so that the nickname 'Trusty Triumph' was quickly applied and stuck fast for evermore.

Triumph's contribution to the British war effort consisted of about 30,000 motor cycles used by despatch riders. The model chosen was the famous Model H, a 550cc single-cylinder side valve with a three-speed gearbox and final belt-drive. For such important work the forces had need of 'trusty' motor cycles and Triumph maintained their reputation.

In the immediate post-war period Lt.-Col. C. V. Holbrook, C.B.E., took over as managing director of the company in the place of the retiring M. J. Schulte, and motor cycle production continued as before. After declining the opportunity to compete in the 1920 Isle of Man T.T. races publicly on a point of principle (the reason being the tendency of manufacturers to make 'specials', which were not representative of their products), Triumph's returned to the fray in 1922. In that year came the first Triumph overhead four valve engine created by Sir Henry Ricardo. A Triumph won second place in the Senior race with Walter Brandish in the saddle, only seven seconds behind the great Alec Bennett on his Sunbeam. The 'Ricardo' also won several speed records at Brooklands and other famous tracks.

During the twenties the Triumph range increased to include a side valve 350cc model, a model P 500cc and a colour change from grey and green paintwork to black with blue panels. It was also during this decade that Triumph motor cars first came into production.

The thirties were a period of change at Triumph's. In the early part of the decade the world financial crisis took its toll and by the middle years it was obvious that Triumph motor cycles would no longer be made unless there was drastic re-organisation. As a result J. Y. Sangster set up the Triumph Engineering Co. Ltd. With Edward Turner, formerly of Ariel, as managing director and chief designer in control, Triumph's continued with renewed zest. The influence of Turner was immediately felt by his introduction of the 'Tiger' range of 250cc, 350cc and 500cc singles, called respectively the Tiger 70, the Tiger 80 and the Tiger 90. In 1938 a 500cc vertical twin-cylinder engined machine called the Speed Twin was introduced, which was so successful that it altered the whole trend of motor cycle engine design throughout the world. It was widely copied and in updated form is still in production by Triumph today, thirty-five years later – a record surely equalled only by Volkswagen. For 1939 a sports version of the 'Speed Twin' was put into production called the Tiger 100.

With the start of the Second World War, the factory immediately turned its machinery to war work, but the German air 'blitz' on Coventry reduced the factory to rubble. The company transferred activities to premises in Warwick and started making spare parts for service machines, gradually progressing to making complete motor cycles again. The Meriden works were ready by 1942 and these premises have continued to be the home of Triumph's since that date. One war development was the adoption of the vertical twin-cylinder engine for use in driving a 6 K.W. (D.C.) auxiliary generator set for the Air Ministry, and many were manufactured for this purpose before the end of hostilities.

After the war Triumph's continued with a policy of twin-cylinder models, and the company prospered with orders rushing in from both home and abroad. Motor cycle demand in both Europe and the United States was high in early post-war years and Triumph's were particularly popular. In the United States Triumph success mainly centred round the Speed Twin with its high mobility compared with American motor cycles in production at that time.

The great innovation of early post-war years was the 650cc Thunderbird, brought into production in 1950. It was renowned for speed and high performance from the beginning, proved by the 214 m.p.h. run of Johnnie Allen on the Utah Salt Flats in the USA in 1956.

In between these years there had been further re-organisation with the Triumph Engineering Company being taken over by B.S.A. in 1951, but continuing to produce motor cycles under its own marque. Examples of new Triumph models in the new era were the 150cc overhead valve single-cylinder Terrier produced from about 1954 and the little 200cc Tiger Cub. The feminine touch was applied with the introduction in the mid-fifties of the 'Tigress' motor scooter.

The 224·57 m.p.h. world speed record was claimed by Triumph's in the early sixties at Bonneville Salt Flats in Utah, USA. Bill Johnson achieved this remarkable speed on a 650cc Triumph Bonneville in 1962. By 1969 the Bonneville became the first production machine to lap the Isle of Man T.T. course at more than 100 m.p.h., and during the same season was awarded the F.I.M. Coupe d'Endurance for production machine racing.

The year before, in 1968, an important Triumph model had been announced, the Triumph Trident 750cc, setting the pace again with an original three-cylinder motor cycle. The Trident has performed with considerable success both on the roads and in competition. Triumphs over the years have also made their name in the trials world. For the man in the street Triumph motor cycles have been daily brought to his attention as the mounts of the British police and of other police forces elsewhere, which indicates their reliability and performance. By the time of publication it is hoped that Triumph production will have moved its base to Birmingham under the umbrella company of Norton Villiers Triumph. Only time will reveal the success or failure of this venture, but the name Triumph will be remembered as long as motor cycles are made and ridden.

45   TRUMP

The Trump motor cycle had a comparatively short life between the years 1906 and 1923. It was originally built by Angus Maitland (a man who also had a close interest in the manufacturing of motor cars and cyclecars) and his cousin Frank A. McNab. Maitland and McNab's first factory, later called Trump Motors Ltd., was opened in Surrey, in South-East England, and produced the Trump-J.A.P. cycle with J.A.P. engines. The Trump-J.A.P.s were mainly single-cylinder machines ranging from 250cc to 500cc, but a few big twins were also built. Since the young founders were keenly interested in racing the early Trump-J.A.P.s were designed for speed. In the first decade of this century, the maximum limit for racing motor cycles was 1000cc, although the reason for this limit is still a mystery. The standard was certainly not set by the Isle of Man T.T. races which were first classified by whether a machine was a single- or twin-cylinder. Trump-J.A.P.s were most successful in road races, especially in the hands of McNab who had many race successes at Brooklands. In a stunt race against an aeroplane the finish was so close that the record books are divided as to who was the winner. Earlier in 1909, a 500cc Trump-J.A.P. created a track record when covering forty-eight miles in an hour. Their road racing successes did not stretch to the T.T. races where on the only occasion Trumps were entered, namely in the solitary 1910 event, both machines were forced to retire.

The early Trumps were characterised by their braced steering-heads and the 'big tube' situated just behind the engine. The long, narrow petrol tank was specially designed for racing purposes. In order to ensure minimum loss of time in refuelling. the petrol cap was closed by a coil spring fixed to the tank floor. The oil tank, as on many racing machines of that period, was fixed on top of the petrol tank. The '90 bore' overhead valve engine introduced in about 1910 proved the most successful. Another significant Trump feature was their comparative lightness since the 1000cc model weighed in at an almost insignificant 220 pounds.

Maitland left Trumps in 1911 to carry on his own business elsewhere, while the organisation continued making motor cycles for another twelve years, latterly in a factory based in Birmingham.

Despite a relatively short existence Trumps could claim royal support, for in 1922 the Duke of York owned a Trump-Anzani which was ridden in competitive events by S. E. Wood, including races at the famous Brooklands track. In fact, the Essex Motor Club ran a charity meeting at Brooklands in that same year and the Duke was present to watch his machine perform.

46 VAUXHALL

The name Vauxhall is mainly associated with the famous motor car, and indeed the firm, which dabbled with two-wheelers in the 1920s, never came to satisfactory terms with motor cycle production. Major Halford, who was responsible for the celebrated Napier 'Sabre' engine used in the Hawker 'Tempest' fighter aircraft, was the designer for the first Vauxhall motor cycle. It was an ambitious project and the machine would have been perhaps the most technically advanced motor cycle on the road, but the fact that it would also have been the most expensive may well have prompted the decision not to go into production. With only twelve engines and less than half that number of frames ready the company decided to sell off the only two completed machines, which were made in 1922, and cut their losses. Both were sold to employees for about £45. The net result was that the purchasers were in the happy position of owning rare motor cycles, and, in the not-so-happy position of having to find the rare spare parts when some mechanical failure occurred. The answer was that if a spare could not be found, it had to be made by the owner. It is therefore all the more remarkable that a Vauxhall motor cycle is still being ridden on the roads today. The credit must go to R. D. (Bob) Thomas, a Vintage Motor Cycle Club enthusiast, who obtained possession of a Vauxhall motor cycle in about 1950 when it had lain stripped and in boxes for over twenty years.

Many parts were missing, others needed repair, and all needed cleaning and painting. Undaunted, Mr Thomas set about the task, which included the manufacture of the main frame, petrol tank, handlebars, exhaust system and clutch. It took over twelve years of his life to renovate this machine but he considers it all worth while. He still rides it today having passed the thousand-mile mark. The top speed recorded is about 82 m.p.h. but he claims the machine will cruise at 50 m.p.h.

The Vauxhall was certainly different from its British contemporaries. It was the first British four-cylinder shaft-driven motor cycle and had the remarkable feature of fully interchangeable wheels. The engine has four separate cast-iron cylinders with fixed heads and parallel push-rod operated overhead valves giving 30 b.h.p. The engine, gearbox and clutch are housed in one complete unit and the clutch is operated with a foot control. There are three gears with two selectors, again an unusual feature. The frame carrying the large engine unit is of duplex cradle type with a detachable tube to allow the gearbox and clutch to be taken out for repairs and maintenance. The silencer is a casting under the left foot-board and the tool box is another casting of similar shape under the right one.

A propeller shaft transmits power to the wheel. There are indeed many features more common to motor cars than motor cycles, including flutes on the fuel tank, but the only Vauxhall motor cycle now known to be in existence still gives much pleasure to its owner and rider.

47 VELOCETTE

The firm of Veloce Ltd., formed in 1905 by Johann Goodman, was a family concern, which included his sons Percy, Eugene and daughter Ethel and grandsons Bertram and Peter, and made history in the motor cycle world by producing exceedingly high-grade machines.

Veloce were always a leading design force, and the famous overhead camshaft engine produced in 1924 was to win innumerable races between then and 1950.

The first machines of note were lightweights to satisfy the demand which existed in the years prior to the First World War. After that the 250 two-stroke models were highly competitive and in the top-grade lightweight class.

The Goodmans always concentrated on sound engineering principles and the little pre-war lightweights demonstrated this clearly. The two-speed gear, chain-drive machines were very advanced. When production re-commenced in 1919 the two-speed two-stroke first incorporated the characteristic de-saxe offset crankshaft. It is interesting to note that a ladies' model was offered, with provision in the dropped tube frame for the adequate skirts worn in this period. One-piece crankcases were used with a single bearing crankshaft until 1926, after which the more conventional split crankcases were adopted with bearings at both ends of the crankshaft. The sports two-strokes were developed to exceed 70 miles per hour, and performed admirably in the T.T. races in this immediate post-war period. In 1921 they finished 3rd, 5th and 7th in the 250cc class of the Junior and again 3rd in the first Lightweight race.

In 1924, Percy Goodman started work on one of the most famous motor cycle engines of all time, a 350cc overhead camshaft model K, destined to win many T.T.s, Grand Prix races, and innumerable races in the hands of private owners.

This new machine was on exhibition at the 1924 show at Olympia as a Veloce and attracted much attention. Since it was common practice in pre-war days to add 'ette' to lightweight machines, such as Levisette, Zenette, etc., dealers insisted on the name Velocette being used.

As the prototype went through major development in the winter of 1924 and early 1925, the production models which first left the factory in July of that year differed substantially from the show version. To cope with the demand for the new model, as well as for the popular two-strokes, a new factory was necessary and the move was made to the Humphries and Dawes works, home of O.K. motor cycles. The winning of the 1926 Junior T.T. and seven subsequent T.T. races and Grands Prix have endeared the make to motor cyclists the world over. The first 'K's were fitted with Druid forks, but a year later Webbs products replaced them. A small batch of roadster models with Dowty telescopic forks was built in about 1948.

The Velocette policy of offering their successful racing products to the public was popular, particularly in 1929 when the replica race winning model was available as a 'KTT' to private owners. They made full use of these excellent machines in all types of speed events.

Apart from the Goodman family, one name stands out more than others in the development of the machines, the late Harold Willis, whose keen sense of humour is still remembered. Possibly his most important single unit was the excellent positive stop foot-change device, devised when hand change was the order of the day.

Alec Bennet became the first famous rider to win a T.T. on a Velocette, other riders being Frank Longman, Freddie Frith, and Stanley Woods. At Brooklands in 1928, F. G. Hicks won the 350 sidecar class in the 200-mile race at 70·84 m.p.h., and a solo took the hour record at 100·39 with Harold Willis in the saddle. This was the first 350cc motor cycle to break the hundred barrier for the coveted 'hour'.

Speedway was catered for in a year when most manufacturers offered a 'dirt track model' at the show of 1929. The new model offered a modified frame with lateral strengthening, special forks, countershaft only and a 'bored' out (82mm) 350, with a standard stroke of 81 and high compression piston for use with methanol, giving a capacity of 411cc. This did not prove successful as most manufacturers discovered, with the exception of Rudge and Douglas who for a spell were supreme in this type of racing.

Many are confused by the engine prefix on Velocettes. All the OHC models are K. The following letters denote the model, for example, KSS meant Super Sports model or variations in specification, while KTT indicated T.T. Replicas, KTS-Touring Sports, and so on. All 'M's' are push-rod overhead valve models.

The depression demanded an economy model in 1930. This was a modified K with coil ignition, full equipment and a two-port head, all popular items but, even at a competitive price, this was not the answer. The model was therefore dropped in favour of a high camshaft 250 o.h.v. in 1934, starting the 'M' range – the 'MOV', to be followed by a larger version a little later, the 350, which became the MAC. Three-speed gearboxes were used up to 1932 on the 'K' models; thereafter the four-speed boxes of similar basic design were fitted to all models.

The late 1930s brought more interesting designs in prototype form, such as the model O, an overhead valve vertical twin built as a super touring machine, while for racing a supercharged 500cc twin appeared nick-named 'The Roarer'. Development of both these models was stopped by the war.

The machine adopted by the War Office was a modified MAC, designated MAF and many of these models gave useful service under the difficult conditions of war.

After hostilities, production was resumed with both K and M ranges but by 1949 the Ks were discontinued – a wonderful span of twenty-four years for a design still successful in races to the end.

Modified 'M' types brought up to date with short-stroke motors as Venom and Vipers proved popular until production ceased.

The LE (little engine) was a winner from the start, despite many teething troubles. This was a horizontally-opposed side valve and water-cooled, shaft-drive twin of 150cc, enlarged almost immediately to 200cc. There was full protection for the rider, and also the great asset of easy starting by hand lever, which could not fail to attract utility riders.

This machine was almost universally adopted by police forces throughout the country and overseas, and enjoyed a production run of some sixteen years.

A 200cc sports version was offered in 1956 and was produced until about

1961, basically consisting of the unit construction crankcase gearbox unit and shaft-drive of the LE, but with overhead valves and air-cooled cylinders in a tubular frame. It was certainly a delightful little bike to ride, but, owing to its small 200cc engine, it was on the whole over-driven and suffered extinction.

The last impressive proof of performance was in March, 1961, when a 500 Venom Clubman, the push-rod o.h.v., successfully attacked the 24-hour record at Montlhery, averaging 100·05 m.p.h. which included the 12-hour record at the astonishing average speed of 104·66 m.p.h. This was the first machine to top 'the ton' for a day and at the time of writing it still holds the 24-hours record in the 500cc class.

The factory closed down in 1971 with the family of Goodmans still in charge, a wonderful record of production of high-class motor cycles, bettered by none.

48 WOOLER

The 'Flying Banana' was a Wooler motor cycle of the early 1920s. John Wooler made his first motor cycle in 1911 and quickly gained a reputation for originality and advanced ideas. His first was a 344cc two-stroke machine with a double-ended piston for the horizontal single cylinder, which eliminated crankcase compression. Even the first Wooler motor cycle was a pioneer of spring frame design. He used a special type of variable pulley gear, where the front pulley swung radially on a quadrant, inside of which one gear was fixed to the crankshaft driving a gear fixed to the variable pulley. This was operated by two pedals and the device reduced belt slip and generally facilitated gear changing.

In the post-war period up to 1926, only 350cc and 500cc models were produced, these being flat twin-cylinder machines. The 350cc models had side exhaust and overhead inlet valves, the 500 had an overhead camshaft. The nickname of 'Flying Banana' was given by Graham Walker to the Wooler after a creditable performance in the Isle of Man T.T. Junior Race of 1921, when it finished in thirty-fourth place. As the elongated bright yellow petrol tank flashed past it drew this analogy from the lips of the enthusiastic observer. The tank was further distinguished by the fact that, unlike most others, it enveloped the steering head at the front of the machine. This particular aspect of the tank was changed by the mid-twenties. An advertising gimmick to emphasise the economy of the Wooler was the claim that the 350cc machine had attained the phenomenal consumption of 311 miles per gallon, a feat that was actually achieved during a special test. Another innovation at Wooler's at this time was a 511cc overhead camshaft single-cylinder model, but very few were made.

It was not often that a Midlands-based motor cycle company was uprooted and brought to London, but this happened when Wooler took over the Packmann and Poppe motor cycle company in the late twenties. The latter were renowned for their clean and quiet motor cycles, as the engines used were the sleeve valve Barr and Stroud, and the machine was called the 'silent three'. Production was continued in Wembley until 1930. That was also the year when Wooler's stopped production for seventeen years as the demand for motor cycles had drastically decreased and the production costs had just as drastically increased. Wooler's put up the shutters until after the Second World War when production started up again for a short period of time. In 1948 Wooler showed a prototype 500cc flat four-cylinder with a complicated crank arrangement based on a Beam engine, which unfortunately was never put into production and not more than two engines were actually made.

The Company continued in business until 1955 making a handful of completely redesigned prototypes, with a more conventional flat four-cylinder overhead valve engine and swinging arm spring frame. Unfortunately only two of these machines have survived.

John Wooler died in 1952 having experimented with motor cycles since 1909 and having complete control of the firm until his death. He was a brilliant engineer with original ideas and worthy of a place in any history of motor cycle pioneers.

49 YAMAHA

This is another Japanese company who in a comparatively short period of time have earned a world-wide reputation for production of high quality two-stroke motor cycles. The first Yamaha motor cycle was in production in 1954 and at the present date the two-stroke range includes machines of 50, 75, 125, 200, 250 and 350cc, whilst the factory is introducing the concept of four-stroke machines of higher cubic capacity. The company claims the first rotary engined motor cycle prototype ever built in the world, the Yamaha Rotary RZ201 which was first shown to the general public at the 1972 Tokyo Motor Show. The motor cycle of the future is being developed at present by the Yamaha engineers. Yamaha were quick to export their machines and have met with particular popularity in Canada and the USA. Apart from success in the streets, Yamaha have also had considerable success on the race tracks, in moto-cross and trials events around the world. Much of their road racing success has been due to riders of the calibre of Phil Read, who in fact collected the first T.T. winners trophy for the company in 1965 in the Lightweight 125cc event. Road racing success has steadily improved at Yamaha and in the early 1970s the factory won the 250cc world road racing championship three years running.

Yamaha have also earned a reputation in another less well-known racing event, ice racing, which is so popular in Scandanavian countries. Certainly Yahama is popular in the cold climates as the Yamaha snowmobile is to be used in the mountain rescue service in Norway. With this knowledge and expertise being applied to the production of motor cycles perhaps Yamaha riders apply their brakes in winter with a little more confidence than other motor cyclists! The reliability of Yamaha was put to the test by S. Shoji of Japan who followed in the tracks of other men before him making the lonely motor cycle trip around the world, starting in 1971 and finishing the trip in twenty-two months covering 73,000 kilometres on his Yamaha 250 DT1. The Yamaha motor cycles appear to have passed these gruelling tests unscarred, and the future seems to offer even more opportunities and challenge for them. No doubt Yamaha will rise to the occasion.

50 ZENITH

Zenith motor cycles were in production from about 1904 until 1950, the machines being manufactured at a variety of factories in or around London. The driving force behind Zenith was their chief designer F. W. (Freddie) Barnes who, apart from being the man responsible for manufacture of frames (which were used in conjunction with the big J.A.P. 1000cc engines for many high speed events), was responsible for the 'Gradua' gear. This gear was devised at the time when motor cycles were belt-driven. The mechanics of the Gradua gear were a variable engine pulley with adjustable effective diameter worked by a handle, with simultaneous correction of the belt length made by sliding the rear wheel backwards or forwards in the rear fork slots. As a solution to gear problems it was very much a 'curates egg'. Its disadvantage was that in the higher ratio range it was of no use, except to the big twin-cylinder machines when travelling exclusively on the level, which in the early years of this century was comparatively rare. Its advantage showed itself most effectively in speed hill climbs, where other machines found themselves limited to a single choice of gear ratio before commencing their ascent. The Zenith rider could change during the journey up, which in the minds of rival riders (and manufacturers) eager for success, was an unfair advantage. The net result was that the Zenith motor cycle with its Gradua gear was barred from entering single-gear classes in speed hill climbs by about fifteen or sixteen leading motor cycle clubs of the day. Quick to spot the publicity value in this unfavoured attribute, the firm took the word *barred* as their trade-mark.

Throughout their production life Zenith used engines made by other companies, chiefly Fafnir and J.A.P. The Zenith 'Bi-Car', propelled by a Fafnir engine, first caused the public to pay attention to the firm. A whole range of Zenith motor cycles from 147cc to 1100cc were manufactured over the years, the small ones powered by Villiers engines, the larger by Bradshaw, Fafnir, Precision and J.A.P. engines. The range of models followed the standard patterns, and eventually in 1950 the lack of independence in engines for their machines finally told. Finding it impossible to obtain suitable engines from outside sources, the firm ceased production.

The name of Zenith was prominent in the results of hill climbs, but the marque will more probably be remembered for its many successes on Brooklands race track. Captain O. M. Baldwin, Joe Wright, G. W. Patchett, T. R. Allchin and H. J. Knight were all notable riders on this make and holders of the Gold Star for lapping Brooklands at over 100 m.p.h. Among his many successes, C. T. Ashby included a victory in the 200-mile sidecar race of 1925, and Joe Wright in the same year took the lap record to 109·9 m.p.h. Both Baldwin and Wright held the Brooklands lap record on many occasions as well as the maximum speed record.